Medieval Realms

1066-1500

J F AYLETT

Hodder & Stoughton
LONDON SYDNEY AUCKLAND TORONTO

ACKNOWLEDGEMENTS

The Publishers would like to thank the following for permission to reproduce material and copyright illustrations in this volume:

Cassell Publishers plc for the extract from *History of the English Speaking Peoples* (1956-8) by Winston Churchill; Times Newspapers Limited for the extract from *The Times*, 2 September 1987.

Aerofilms p14; Photo Alinari p22 right; The Ancient Art and Architecture Collection p30 left, p59; Bayerische Staatsbibliothek Munich p43 left; Bibliotheque Nationale Paris MS FR 2813 F265 p23 top left, p50, p55; The British Library MS COT VIT A XIII f 3v p7, MS FAUST B VIII f 72v p11 left, MS STOWE 17 p13 left, Queen Mary's Psalter p26 left, COTTON MS Claudius BII f341 p28, HARL MS 5102 f17 p29, HARL MS 1319 f57 p33 top, HARL 4375 f140 p39 right, ADD 47682 f34 p40 left, ROYAL MS 10 E IV f222v p40 right, ROYAL MS 18 E I f175 p52, ADD MS 42130 f171 p63 top; The Bodleian Library MS Douce 6 fol 22r p19, MS RAWL D 929 part 4 p21, MS Canon Liturg 347 fol 3v p22 left, MS ASHMOLE 391/V fol 10r p44 left; Janet and Colin Bord p18 top left, p61; Bulloz p16 top left, p35; Cambridge University Collection p48; Martyn Cordey p32; The Master and Fellows of Corpus Christi College Cambridge CCC MS 16 f44v p30 right, CCC MS 61 fr p57, CCC MA 171 f265r p58; The President and Fellows of Corpus Christi College Oxford MS 157 f 382-383 p11 right; English Heritage p6 left; Mary Evans Picture Library p41 left, p51; Sarah Foley p43 right; Giraudon p45; Sonia Halliday Photographs p13 right; Judith Heneghan p49 right; Michael Holford Photographs p2 both, p3, p6 right, p20 both; Holkham Hall HOLKHAM MS 311 (Georgics) p16 bottom right; The Hulton Picture Company p37 top; Novosti p63 bottom; Scala p36, p37 bottom, p46 left; Society of Antiquaries of London p39 left; From Robin of Sherwood an HTV West/Goldcrest production. By permission of HTV/WEST/Aquarius p23 bottom right.

Every effort has been made to trace and acknowledge ownership of copyright.
The publishers will be glad to make suitable arrangements with any copyright holders whom it has not been possible to contact.

For Liz, who found herself back in the middle ages again.

British Library Cataloguing in Publication Data
Aylett, J. F. (John F.)
Medieval realms 1066–1500.
1. Great Britain, 1066–1485
I. Title
942.02

ISBN 0 340 54823 1

First published 1991

Typeset by Litho Link Ltd, Welshpool, Powys
Printed in Hong Kong for the educational publishing division of Hodder and Stoughton Ltd, Mill Road, Dunton Green, Sevenoaks, Kent by Colorcraft Ltd.

CONTENTS

In the 11th century, a monk thought he had found out how to fly. Unfortunately, he was wrong. He tied wings to his hands and feet and flapped his way off the abbey tower. He made it for about 200 metres before crash-landing. He broke both his legs and was lame for life.

He believed his mistake was in not wearing a tail.

We know about events like this mainly through the people who wrote chronicles during the Middle Ages. Often, they were monks themselves. Their aims were to teach, entertain and satisfy people's curiosity. I hope this book does the same.

Highlighted words, such as chronicle, are explained in the glossary on page 64.

1 THE NORMAN CONQUEST

1000 1100 1200 1300 1400 1500

In 1066 there were two **invasions** of England. One of them, by the Normans, was successful. That is why this chapter is called The *Norman Conquest*.

Historians want to find out why things happened. Why did the Normans come here? Why were they successful? Why was 1066 the last time England was conquered? They look for anwers in things written or made at the time. Historians call these *primary sources*. Somewhere, in all the things written at the time, we ought to find the answers.

But it is not as easy as it sounds. The event happened so long ago. Some of the information has been lost. And writers of the time do not always agree on details about the Norman Conquest. However, we will start by seeing what the Normans said about it. This is one of their accounts:

In 1064, an English earl called Harold Godwinson sailed across the Channel to visit Duke William of Normandy. He was sent by King Edward the Confessor, the English king. Edward had no children. So Harold was going to promise that Duke William would become king when Edward died.

Harold stayed awhile with the Normans. He even went out fighting with Duke William. The Normans were impressed by his strength. And, during his visit, he made the promise.

A

This picture shows Harold making his oath. An oath is a solemn promise. Notice that his right hand is touching a box. It contained holy **relics**. This made the oath doubly serious.

B William of Poitiers was a Norman. He described the event in about 1073:

Harold swore an oath of **loyalty** to William. A number of famous men who are not given to lying and were present have told how Harold freely made the following statement: he would act as William's representative, as long as King Edward lived; after Edward's death he would do everything he could to make sure William became King of England.

Two years later, King Edward died. Immediately afterwards, Harold was chosen as king by the leading **nobles**. Duke William felt insulted. After all, Harold had promised to support him. Harold had obviously broken his promise. He had got himself crowned before William could get there. That was why the Normans invaded.

C Harold is crowned. This picture, like sources A and D, comes from the Bayeux Tapestry.

It all seems quite clear, doesn't it? But we must remember that this is what the Normans said. Even the two pictures were made for Normans. What about the English? Did their writers give the same story?

This is where it starts to get difficult! *The Anglo-Saxon Chronicles* are a history written by English monks at about this time. They say nothing at all about Harold's promise to William. Why not? Did the Normans just make it up?

Later, English writers did include the story – but their version was different. They said that Harold had really been trying to rescue two of his relations. Or that William tricked him. Who do we believe?

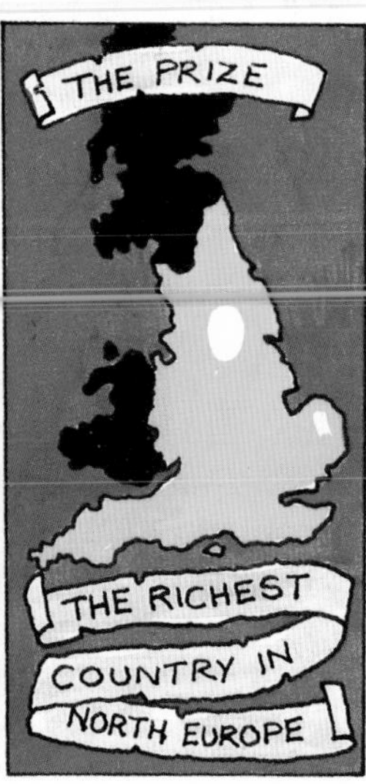

Nowadays, it would be easier to decide. There would be film of the event on television. Reporters would interview Harold and William. But these events took place over 900 years ago. There were no newspapers, no television and no cameras.

Primary sources are things written or made at the time of the event. Primary sources may disagree. Sometimes, the writers do not see things in the same way.

1 Explain the meaning of *primary source* in your own words.

2 Put these events in the order in which they happened: (a) Duke William invaded England; (b) King Edward died; (c) Harold became king; (d) Earl Harold visited William; (e) Harald Hardrada invaded England.

3 a) What is the evidence to show that Harold made an oath?
b) What are the reasons for thinking he didn't make an oath?
c) If Harold did make an oath, why would *The Anglo-Saxon Chronicles* not mention it?
d) Do you think he did or he didn't? Explain how you decided.

In September, the King of Norway, Harald Hardrada, landed in the north with a large army. King Harold marched north and fought them. He won a crushing victory. Hardrada was killed. But, within days, King Harold had bad news.

On 28 September, Duke William's army had landed in Sussex. Now, Harold had to hurry south and find fresh troops. On 14 October, the two armies met just outside Hastings. Like most battles of the time, it would be over before nightfall. The winner would be King of England.

The Bayeux Tapestry

The photographs on these two pages are from the Bayeux Tapestry. This was probably made for William's half-brother Odo, who is shown in the scene below. He was Bishop of Bayeux.

In fact, it is not really a tapestry. It is actually made of wool sewn on linen and is about 70 metres long. It may have been made by English women in the south of England before 1077. Even so, the people who made it probably did not see the events themselves. But an eye-witness probably gave advice.

It has been repaired a lot over the years. Anything in orange, light green or yellow was sewn later and is harder to see. (Look at the arrow in source B on page 6.)

Notice that animals' back legs are usually a different colour from the legs nearer to us. This was because people at this time found it difficult to draw in perspective.

D Soon after the Normans landed. Bishop Odo is blessing the food and drink.

VICTORY AT THE GREY APPLETREE

There were, of course, no guns in 1066. Most fighting was hand-to-hand. Swords with wide blades were the main weapon. The English also used battleaxes which they swung with both hands. They fought on foot.

But the Normans had two great advantages. They had knights mounted on war-horses who were trained to charge the enemy. Meanwhile, archers fired arrows to distract the enemy. The English had few, if any, archers.

At Hastings, the Norman knights did not have much of an enemy to charge. Some of Harold's troops were paid Danish fighters. But quite a few were just Sussex farmers, called out for the emergency. They had no armour – unless you count their straw hats! Their weapons were stones tied to lumps of wood.

The sun rose at about half-past five on 14 October 1066. Harold put his banners in position on a hilltop. The English called it 'the place of the grey appletree'. There, he waited for William to move.

The fighting began at nine o'clock. The English stood their ground against the Norman archers; they cut down the Norman foot-soldiers with their heavy axes.

A This is what a shirt of chain mail looked liked. Each shirt might have 15,000 separate iron rings.

They even coped with the knights. Time and again, the Normans charged the English – only to be beaten back. These charges were led by William and his nobles. They included Bishop Odo. The Church said that priests should not shed blood. So he clubbed people to death instead.

Then, the Normans pretended to retreat. The English made the mistake of following them. The Normans surrounded them and hacked them down. William later repeated the trick.

B The death of Harold, from the Bayeux Tapestry. The Wessex dragon (from Harold's banner) is shown at the top.

Sometime in the late afternoon, Harold himself was killed. As soon as the news got about, many of his men fled. The Normans chased after them, killing everyone they caught. The battle was over. William had won.

Of course, he was not yet king. In fact, the English Council wanted someone else as their new king. An English army even fought William outside London.

So William marched across southern England and back, burning the land as he went. He frightened the English into giving up. That Christmas, in 1066, William was crowned king in Westminster Abbey in London.

1 You are William. Which of the following things would you do next? Give each one marks out of ten. Then, compare your results with someone else's.

- Go back to Normandy.
- Make friends with the English nobles.
- Put up posters so people know you have won.
- Give some English land to your supporters.
- Build good defences.
- Punish the English who fought against you.
- Announce your victory on the radio.

Many historians wrote about the battle. These are just three accounts of Harold's death.

C Matthew of Westminster (a monk) wrote in about 1320:

At last Harold fell after his brain had been split through by an arrow. But while the King was still breathing, one of the Normans ran up to him and cut off his leg. William had him beaten for this, and expelled him from the army.

He sent the body of King Harold to his mother. William did not want the large ransom that she had offered for the body. When she received it, she buried it at Waltham in the church which Harold himself had built.

D Bishop Guy of Amiens. (Historians disagree about when this was written.)

[The Duke] called Eustace to his side. Hugh went with them. The fourth man was Giffard. These four between them brought about the king's death.

With the point of his lance, the first pierced Harold's shield and then his chest, drenching the ground with his blood, which poured out in torrents. The second cut off his head, just below where his helmet protected him.

The third tore his insides out with his javelin. The fourth hacked off his leg at the thigh and hurled it far away. Struck down in this way, his dead body lay on the ground.

E William of Malmesbury: *The History of the Kings of England* (1125).

Receiving the fatal arrow from a distance, he died. One of the soldiers with a sword cut his thigh as he lay. William dismissed him from the service for this shameful and cowardly action.

F This picture shows Duke William personally killing King Harold. It comes from a 14th-century manuscript.

One question historians ask about a source is:

When was it written or made?

Primary sources are made by people who were alive at the time. But some primary sources were written by people who did not actually *see* the events. Two of the writers above definitely did not *see* the battle. Ideally, we would want to know how they found out.

Secondary sources are made long afterwards by people who definitely did not see the events. A secondary source may have been copied from earlier primary sources. Some writers are more careful than others in the way they use evidence.

2 a) For each source, write down whether it is primary or secondary. Explain how you know. (If you are not sure, say why not.)
b) Which writer(s) did not see the battle?

3 a) There are two different versions of how Harold died. What are they?
b) Be careful! Which version does the Bayeux Tapestry support?
c) Is it possible that both versions are correct? Give reasons.
d) The Bayeux Tapestry may be the earliest source. Does this mean it is the correct one? Explain your answer.
e) Work in pairs. If you wanted to be sure how Harold died, what evidence would you look for?

WILLIAM TAKES CONTROL

William was now king. But he ruled a country which did not want him. Twice, people in the north rebelled. Twice, William had to march north and defeat them. In 1070, he led his troops across the north of England, from east to west. They burned all the food and killed the cattle. They tore down houses and destroyed farm tools.

Some survivors starved to death; others were taken as slaves by the Scots. Rotting bodies lay in the roads to be eaten by wolves. William destroyed the north so completely that whole villages stayed empty for over a decade. Some of these areas are still empty even today. This was William's punishment for rebels.

There were well over a million English in England – but never much more than 20,000 Normans. So William needed other ways of keeping the English under control.

King William introduced a curfew. Each night, church bells rang to tell people to go to bed. 'Curfew' comes from the French 'couvre feu' which means 'rake up the fire'.

Many English nobles had died or fled abroad. So William shared out their land among his followers. It was their reward for helping him win the Battle of Hastings.

But William knew this was risky. These new landowners might become too powerful. They might even challenge him. So he kept one-fifth of the land for himself. He also gave one-quarter to the Church.

Some English nobles hung onto their land, but very few. Some of them were women. Harold's sister, Queen Edith, kept hers. Countess Godiva kept hers. But most land went to the Normans. By 1086, only two English nobles still held land; the rest was controlled by Normans. Much of it was now owned by just ten men.

Each Norman noble was given land but it was scattered throughout England. This made it more difficult for him to raise an army to attack William. One of the lucky ones was William's nephew Hugh, often called Hugh the Fat. (He ate so much he could hardly walk!)

The map below shows where William gave Hugh his land. He was given the whole of Chester to defend in case the Welsh attacked. Elsewhere, as you can see, his manors were dotted about. It would have been difficult for him to organise a rebellion.

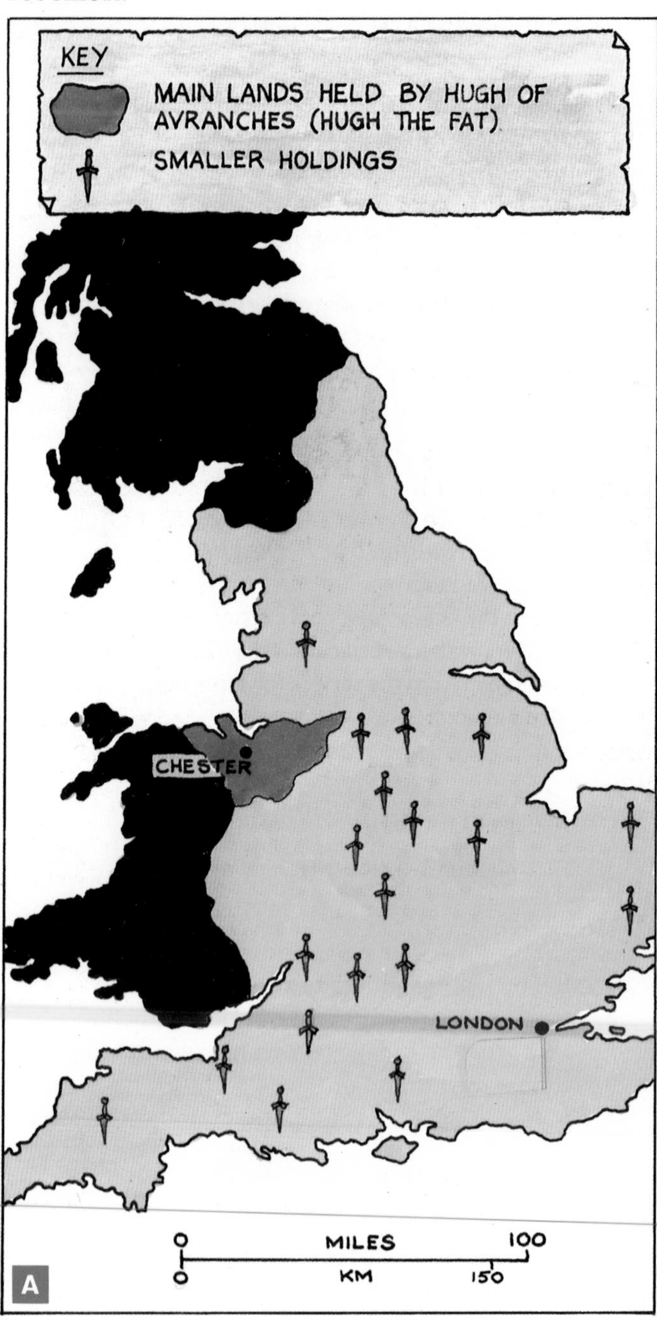

It was expensive for William to defend his new land. Most of his money came from taxes. At Christmas 1085, William announced a plan to find out exactly how much he should be getting. In January 1086, the work began.

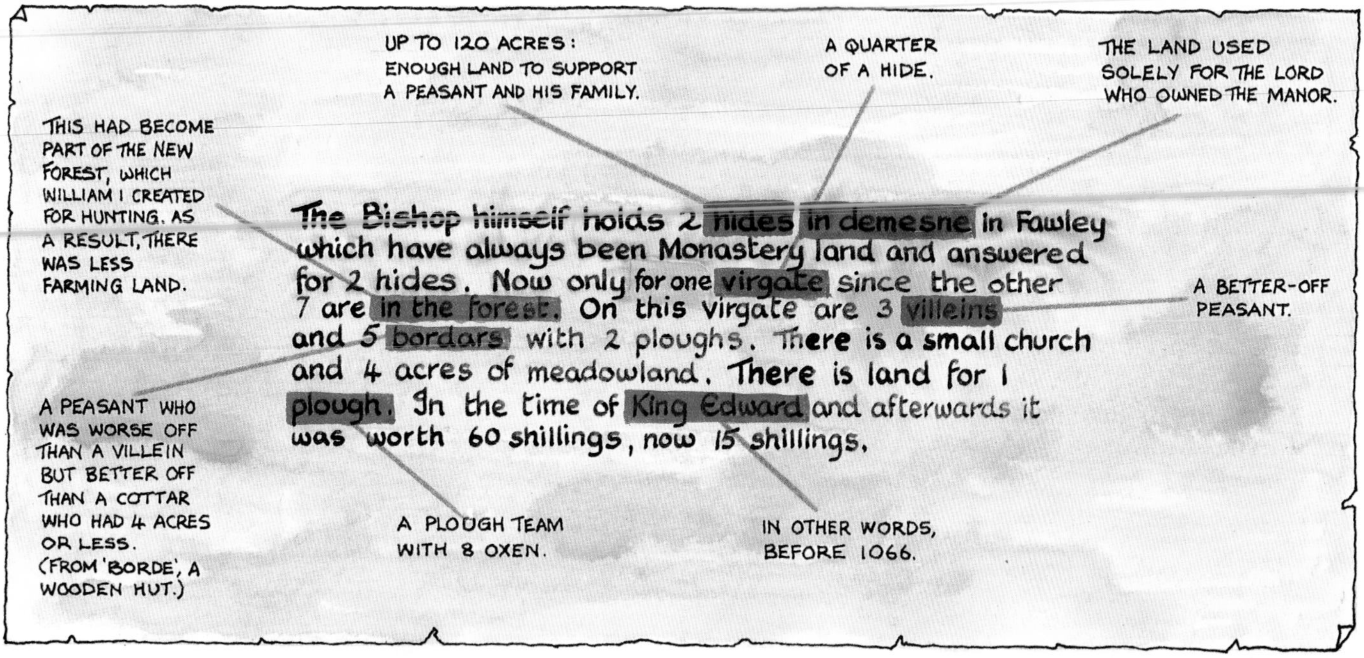

UP TO 120 ACRES: ENOUGH LAND TO SUPPORT A PEASANT AND HIS FAMILY.

A QUARTER OF A HIDE.

THE LAND USED SOLELY FOR THE LORD WHO OWNED THE MANOR.

THIS HAD BECOME PART OF THE NEW FOREST, WHICH WILLIAM I CREATED FOR HUNTING. AS A RESULT, THERE WAS LESS FARMING LAND.

The Bishop himself holds 2 hides in demesne in Fawley which have always been Monastery land and answered for 2 hides. Now only for one virgate since the other 7 are in the forest. On this virgate are 3 villeins and 5 bordars with 2 ploughs. There is a small church and 4 acres of meadowland. There is land for 1 plough. In the time of King Edward and afterwards it was worth 60 shillings, now 15 shillings.

A BETTER-OFF PEASANT.

A PEASANT WHO WAS WORSE OFF THAN A VILLEIN BUT BETTER OFF THAN A COTTAR WHO HAD 4 ACRES OR LESS. (FROM 'BORDE', A WOODEN HUT.)

A PLOUGH TEAM WITH 8 OXEN.

IN OTHER WORDS, BEFORE 1066.

B The Domesday entry for Redbridge Hundred in Hampshire. The book is made of parchment from sheep skins. Up to 1,000 sheep were needed to make it. Redbridge was worth 75p in 1086. The whole of England was valued at £73,000. This made it the richest country in northern Europe!

Officials set out to every part of the kingdom. Each asked exactly the same questions of the people who lived there. The answers were sent to Winchester where a single monk wrote it all down. It took him perhaps eight months to list the details of all 13,418 places which were visited.

Meanwhile, a second set of officials was busy checking the answers. They were making sure that the book was correct. Liars were severely punished. It was the most complete record of any country at that time. The King would know exactly what his land was worth. No wonder they called it the 'King's Book'.

What is the name of the manor?
Who held it in the time of Edward the Confessor?
After 1066? Now, in 1086?
How many hides, then and now?
How many plough-teams, on the lord's farm-lands belonging to the sub-tenants?
How many freemen, villeins, bordars, cottars and slaves – then and now?
How much woodland, meadow, pasture?
How many mills? How many fisheries?
How much was it all worth? How much is it worth now?

These were the questions which people were asked.

We do not know if William ever saw it. He died at dawn on a Thursday morning in September 1087. But his book survived. Within 100 years, people were calling it the Domesday Book. 'Domesday' means 'Day of Judgement'. Any dispute about land could be judged by reading the book.

Putting dates in chronological order means putting them in order, with the earliest date first.

1 a) Write each of these dates on a separate line in chronological order: 1066, 1087, 1085, 1070, 1086.
b) Beside each date, write down what happened in that year.
c) Four of these events showed William's power over the English. Which one did not?

2 William I kept England under control in various ways. How did each of these help:
a) destroying the north of England
b) giving land to his followers
c) splitting up his followers' land
d) introducing a curfew
e) making the Domesday Book?

3 Please work in groups. You have the task of making a Domesday Book for modern Britain. You want to find out what the country is worth now.
a) Write down a list of questions you would ask.
b) Make a note of the reasons why some of your questions are different to those on the left.
c) Make a presentation of your findings.

THE FEUDAL SYSTEM

William needed his Norman barons to help keep the English under control. But he also needed to keep the barons under control. We call the system he used the Feudal system . *Feudum* is a Latin word meaning *land*.

Under the system, even the greatest lords had to accept William as their overlord . Although King William granted land to his barons, he still owned it. So even the greatest lords in England were just his tenants . These rich people were called tenants-in-chief because the King had personally given them land.

Tenants, of course, must pay rent. Very little of this was in cash. Coins were quite rare then. Most of the rent was paid in goods or services.

Once he had his land, a baron gave some of it to his knights. In return, of course, he expected rent. So the knights had to make promises to the barons.

So far, so good. This system made sure that William could always call up about 5,000 knights when he needed them. But someone had to farm the land to grow the food. The knight had no intention of doing the farming himself. So, in turn, he shared out much of his land with the peasants . In return for their land, the peasants, of course, had to pay rent.

It does not sound a very good deal for the peasants. But, in return, they did receive some land. Without it, they could not grow food. And their lord had to protect them, if the village were attacked. Food and safety were most important to the peasants.

King William, however, was worried. The knights did not promise to obey him; they promised to obey the barons. So the barons might just use the knights to revolt against the King.

This had already happened to William in Normandy. He did not want it to happen again. So, in 1086, William called all his knights to Salisbury Plain. Then he made them promise to be loyal to him first – and to their barons second.

A William's nephew, Alain, promises to be loyal to the King in this 13th-century painting from an English history book. Compare this picture of William with source A on page 4.

B The *Holkham Deed* recorded the rent which one villein had to pay in the 13th century. (12d = 5p in modern money.)

Hervey de Monte holds 18 acres for 22d rent at 4 times of payment and 4 hens and does 3 half days weeding and 3 boon-works in autumn at the lord's board and does 1 boon-work with a plough, if he has a horse, at the lord's board . . .

If the lord comes to the [manor] he lends him a horse if he has one to carry bread and goes twice to the lord's mill pond and carries the lord's corn in autumn for one day, if he has a horse.

The first job of an historian is to understand the sources. Sometimes, this is difficult because they are written in an old-fashioned way. Next, he or she must ask questions like these:

- Who wrote or made this?
- When did they do it?
- How reliable is it?

C Norman kings were always afraid of rebellions. These pictures show Henry I having nightmares. (From a chronicle, drawn by a monk in about 1130.)

1 Explain the meanings of each of these terms: feudal system; tenant-in-chief; loyalty; knight. Please work in small groups for the other questions.

2 a) Read source B. Write down each service Hervey had to give. Which do you think he found worst? Give reasons for your choice.
b) Which do you think he found least annoying? Again, give reasons.

3 a) Draw this grid in your book.

	Who made it?	When?	How reliable?
A			
C			

b) Fill in the first two columns about the pictures on this page as fully as possible. (Put 'don't know' if you cannot decide.)
c) Now, give each source a mark out of ten, depending on how reliable you think it is. *Read the captions carefully before you start.*

CASTLES

Castles were few and far between in 1066 when William arrived. By the year 1100, the Normans had built over 500 of them. Castles were a good way of reminding the English who was in control.

From these castles, the Normans could control their new lands. A castle was a base for attacking areas nearby. It also kept the owner safe from an attack by knights on horseback.

The English did the building. Earth was heaped up quickly. In Oxford, for example, soil was just piled on top of people's homes. At Norwich and Cambridge, they knocked the houses down. So, castles were quick to build. The one at York probably took just eight days to put up.

This drawing shows an early motte and bailey castle. A wooden fort stands on the motte. The bailey is the open area nearby. It includes all sorts of other wooden buildings, such as a kitchen. A wooden fence protects it.

The castle was built for defence, not comfort. Some early castles were even more basic than this one. They were really just enclosures. The motte was added later.

However, there is no such thing as a typical motte and bailey castle. Each one was different. Each was built to defend an area against the English. So each had to be designed separately to do the job.

Wooden castles were fine if you wanted to build quickly. (You could not build a stone castle on a fresh mound of earth.) However, they were not completely safe. Fires could start by accident. Or an enemy could fire burning arrows at it. In any case, wood rots.

In the 12th century, there was less risk of rebellion. So the Normans could spend time on improving their castles. These pictures show the changes they made.

Stone keeps look pretty solid. Yet attackers could pound away at the walls with a mangonel, as in the picture below. It was like a huge catapult and slung heavy stones at the walls. (It was also used to 'fire' dead animals – or to return a captured messenger!)

B

However, this did not always work. In 1215, King John was attacking Rochester Castle in Kent. He had five machines throwing stones at the walls, but got nowhere. Not surprising, with walls 3.5 metres thick! (Compare this with the width of your classroom.)

So he hit on a new plan, as this source explains.

C The *Barnwell Chronicle* (13th century).

Expert miners cut their way under the ground, until at last they were under one of the great corner turrets. As they moved soil and rock out, they put wooden beams in, with pit props under them, to hold up the roof above their heads.

They worried every time the beams creaked from the great weight above them. The defenders worried too. In the quiet night, they could hear tapping sounds under the ground but they could do nothing to stop them.

After two months, the miners came out. Brushwood and branches were carried in, as well as fat from 'forty of the fattest pigs of the sort least good for eating'. Then they were set on fire.

The fire crackled and sizzled as all the timbers caught fire and blazed until they collapsed. With a roar the roof gave way. Down came the soil and rock, the castle walls cracked and then the whole turret fell down. After this, few cared to put their trust in castles.

. . . so people built *round* towers instead. Even so, the defenders were not wholly safe. Attackers could build tall wooden towers called siege towers. These were rolled up to the castle walls. Attackers would then fight their way on to the battlements.

Historians study changes in the past. They try to discover what caused these changes.

D A siege tower.

What was needed was a way of keeping attackers at a distance. From about 1250 onwards, castle builders thought they had found the answer . . . they added a moat!

1 The following sentences may be true or false. Write out any true ones and correct any false ones.
a) Early motte and bailey castles were built of wood.
b) In the 12th century, all castles in England and Scotland were built of stone.
c) Early Norman castles always had a motte.
d) Stone keeps were safer than wooden ones.
e) Moats kept attackers at a distance.

2 Work out the answers to these questions.
a) Why were early castles built of wood?
b) Why were stone ones better?
c) Why was a gatehouse added to the castle?
d) Why would anyone 'fire' a dead animal into a castle?
e) Why were later castles built with round towers?

3 Please work in groups. You are attacking a round stone keep. It has a bailey beside it. The whole area is surrounded by a stone wall and a moat. Write down your plan for attacking it. You could sketch it, too.

CASTLES IN THE LATER MIDDLE AGES

Change does not happen everywhere at the same time. When the first stone keeps were being built in England, wooden motte and bailey castles were still being built in Scotland.

Soon after the arrival of moats, knights brought back new ideas of castle-building from the east. The result was a new kind of castle. We call it the concentric castle.

Beaumaris Castle (below) is an example of one of them. Concentric means *with one circle inside another one*. So these castles had two or three rings of castle walls.

A

The inner ring was the real fortress, with its high walls. Anyone getting inside the outer walls could still be fired down on from the inner walls. There was also an extra defence outside the main gates. This is called a **barbican**.

These new castles were not cheap to build. Beaumaris cost £7,000 in the 1290s. That's worth over a million pounds in modern money.

These new castles provided comfortable homes for the lord and his family. Gone was the cold, miserable life inside the early motte and bailey. More rooms were added. There were now separate bedrooms for the lord's family, instead of a dormitory for all.

Yet, within a century, castles were losing their importance. They had been built for defence. Now came an invention which meant that, however strong they were, they were not wholly safe. In the 1300s, the cannon arrived.

In fact, these early cannon did not do much harm. They were not reliable. They were more likely to kill the gunners who fired them than knock down a castle.

Despite cannon, people went on building castles. In fact, by 1400, castles had become so strong that no weapon could destroy them.

A siege was the best way of making the defenders give up. But it was a long and costly job besieging a castle. You could wait years for the people inside to starve. So attackers stopped bothering. Instead of attacking castles, the army marched straight past.

By the 15th century, warfare was changing. Many knights no longer went to fight for their king each year. They paid the king a fine instead. The king used this money to pay soldiers to do the fighting. Disputes were now settled in battles in the open countryside. Archers, they found, were even better in the open than firing from a castle.

As a result, castles were no longer needed for defence. So lords built new ones of brick, not stone. They were not made for defence, but for comfort. The Englishman's castle had become a real home.

However, in the north of England, castle-building went on. Local lords needed to defend themselves from the Scots. The Scottish and Irish lords were still building tower houses long after the English and Welsh stopped using castles for defence.

1 a) Put these changes in castle-building in the order they happened: (i) concentric castles; (ii) stone and shell keeps; (iii) wooden motte and bailey castles; (iv) brick castles; (v) moats.
b) For each change, explain why it happened.
c) This page gives two examples of changes not occurring at the same time in Scotland as in England. What are they?
d) Choose one of these changes. Explain why it happened at different times.

2 a) In pairs, look at the picture on page 15. Early wooden castles were very different to this stone one. Write down as many differences as you can think of.
b) As a group, compare your answers.

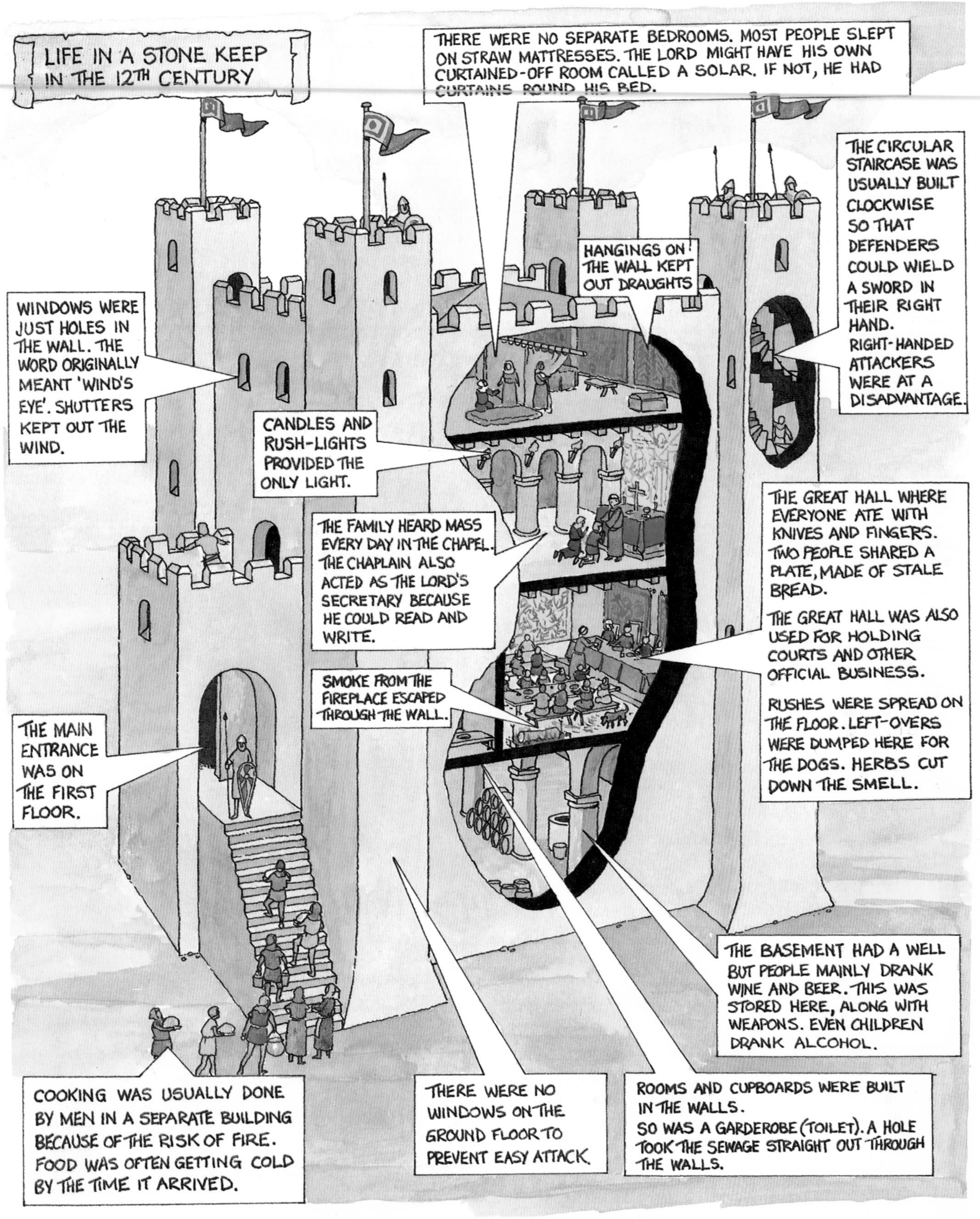

LIFE IN A STONE KEEP IN THE 12TH CENTURY
THERE WERE NO SEPARATE BEDROOMS. MOST PEOPLE SLEPT ON STRAW MATTRESSES. THE LORD MIGHT HAVE HIS OWN CURTAINED-OFF ROOM CALLED A SOLAR. IF NOT, HE HAD CURTAINS ROUND HIS BED.
THE CIRCULAR STAIRCASE WAS USUALLY BUILT CLOCKWISE SO THAT DEFENDERS COULD WIELD A SWORD IN THEIR RIGHT HAND. RIGHT-HANDED ATTACKERS WERE AT A DISADVANTAGE.
HANGINGS ON THE WALL KEPT OUT DRAUGHTS
WINDOWS WERE JUST HOLES IN THE WALL. THE WORD ORIGINALLY MEANT 'WIND'S EYE'. SHUTTERS KEPT OUT THE WIND.
CANDLES AND RUSH-LIGHTS PROVIDED THE ONLY LIGHT.
THE FAMILY HEARD MASS EVERY DAY IN THE CHAPEL. THE CHAPLAIN ALSO ACTED AS THE LORD'S SECRETARY BECAUSE HE COULD READ AND WRITE.
THE GREAT HALL WHERE EVERYONE ATE WITH KNIVES AND FINGERS. TWO PEOPLE SHARED A PLATE, MADE OF STALE BREAD.
THE GREAT HALL WAS ALSO USED FOR HOLDING COURTS AND OTHER OFFICIAL BUSINESS.
RUSHES WERE SPREAD ON THE FLOOR. LEFT-OVERS WERE DUMPED HERE FOR THE DOGS. HERBS CUT DOWN THE SMELL.
SMOKE FROM THE FIREPLACE ESCAPED THROUGH THE WALL.
THE MAIN ENTRANCE WAS ON THE FIRST FLOOR.
THE BASEMENT HAD A WELL BUT PEOPLE MAINLY DRANK WINE AND BEER. THIS WAS STORED HERE, ALONG WITH WEAPONS. EVEN CHILDREN DRANK ALCOHOL.
COOKING WAS USUALLY DONE BY MEN IN A SEPARATE BUILDING BECAUSE OF THE RISK OF FIRE. FOOD WAS OFTEN GETTING COLD BY THE TIME IT ARRIVED.
THERE WERE NO WINDOWS ON THE GROUND FLOOR TO PREVENT EASY ATTACK.
ROOMS AND CUPBOARDS WERE BUILT IN THE WALLS.
SO WAS A GARDEROBE (TOILET). A HOLE TOOK THE SEWAGE STRAIGHT OUT THROUGH THE WALLS.

2 VILLAGE LIFE

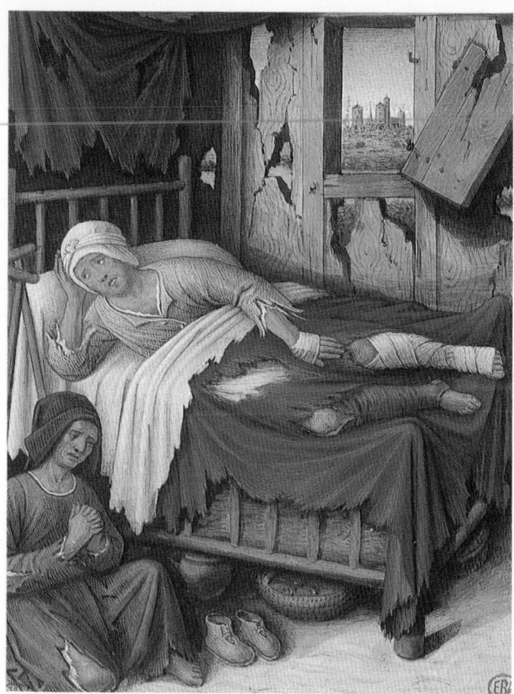

A A French picture of a peasant's cottage in about 1490.

We have seen that each castle was different. The same was true of the villages beyond the castle walls. Of course, most were now owned by Normans. But food still had to be grown – and villagers went on growing it much as they had done before.

Throughout southern England and the Midlands, villagers grew their crops in vast open fields. Many villages had three of these fields. But some had two; others had four.

Here, the villagers grew their crops in strips. Each family had some of these strips in each field. They were scattered about. That way, nobody got all the good land or all the bad land. The lord, too, had strips in these fields, as well as his own separate land.

You cannot keep growing the same crops on the same land unless you add goodness to the soil. So each year the villagers grew a different crop in each field. The main crops were wheat and rye (for bread), barley (for beer), oats (for porridge or animal food) and beans (for soups and stews). Most of these crops had one thing in common – they filled you up!

Each year one field was left *fallow*. This means that no seeds were planted in it. Instead, animals were allowed to graze on the weeds which grew there. Medieval farmers had no fertilizers – so the animals did it for them.

A team of oxen pulled the heavy plough across the fields. It is hard work keeping oxen going. About 220 yards (200 metres) is the furthest anyone can manage. So 220 yards became the standard length of a strip. 220 yards is a furlong. The word means *furrow long*.

People often think of these strips as being neat straight lines, but they were not. As the oxen reached the end of a strip, the ploughman slowly swung them round. The result is an 'S' shape which curves backwards.

Everyone in the village had to share this work. Each year, one villager was chosen to be the reeve. It was his job to organise the work. Everyone had to do the same job at the same time.

The villagers grew all the food they ate, often with little to spare. If the weather was bad, so was the crop. In a really bad year, they starved. In 1316, many villagers had to eat dogs and rats. They had no choice. They could not just nip out to Tesco for a tin of spaghetti. There were no shops – or tins, or spaghetti!

As time passed, villagers chopped down more and more of the woods. More land was needed for food. In 1086, the population of England was between 1.5 and 2 million people. By 1340, the figure was nearly 4 million.

B Life on the farm is shown in this 14th-century picture.

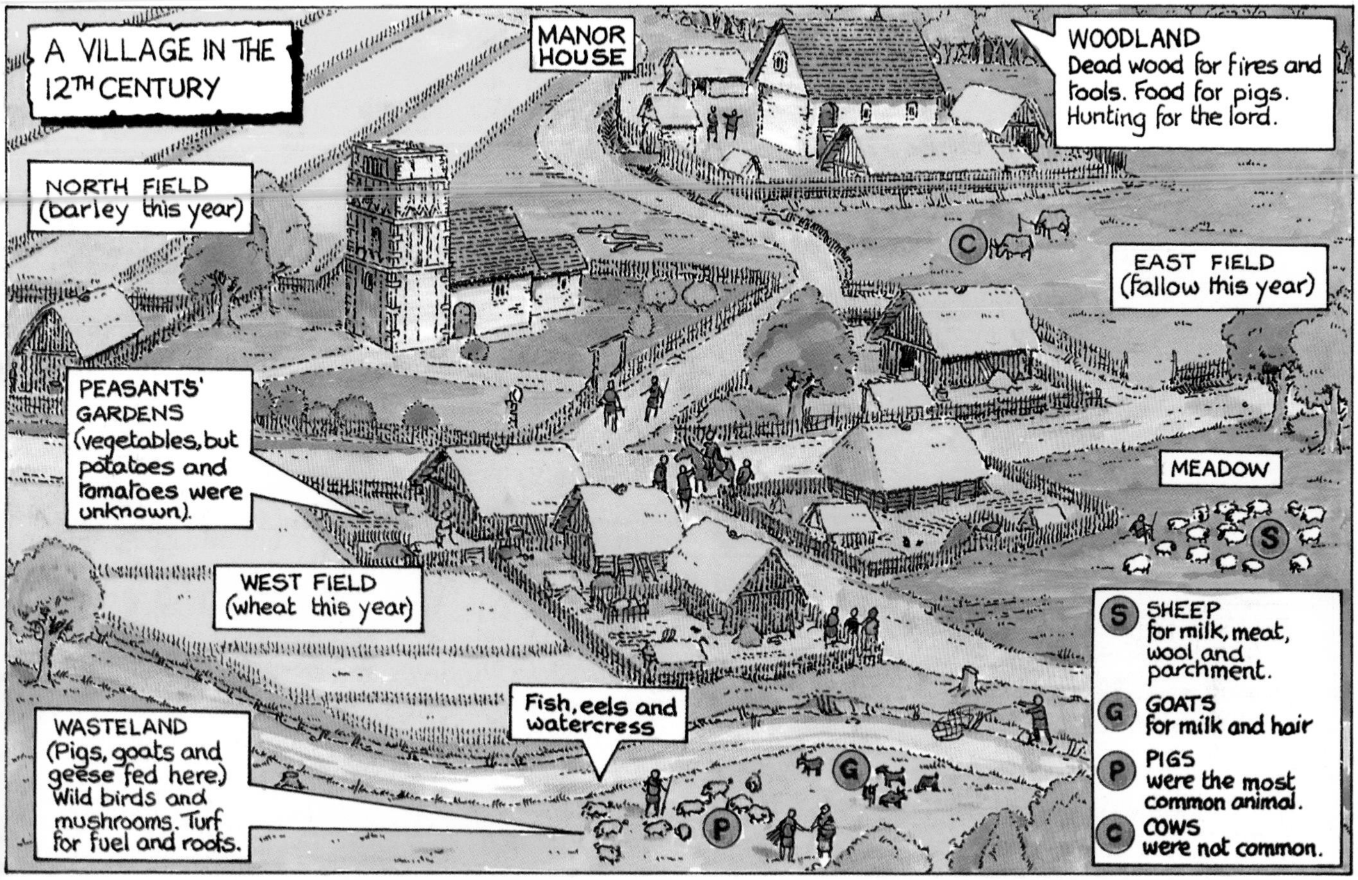

A VILLAGE IN THE 12TH CENTURY

MANOR HOUSE

WOODLAND
Dead wood for fires and tools. Food for pigs. Hunting for the lord.

NORTH FIELD
(barley this year)

EAST FIELD
(fallow this year)

PEASANTS' GARDENS
(vegetables, but potatoes and tomatoes were unknown).

MEADOW

WEST FIELD
(wheat this year)

Fish, eels and watercress

WASTELAND
(Pigs, goats and geese fed here) Wild birds and mushrooms. Turf for fuel and roofs.

S SHEEP for milk, meat, wool and parchment.
G GOATS for milk and hair
P PIGS were the most common animal.
C COWS were not common.

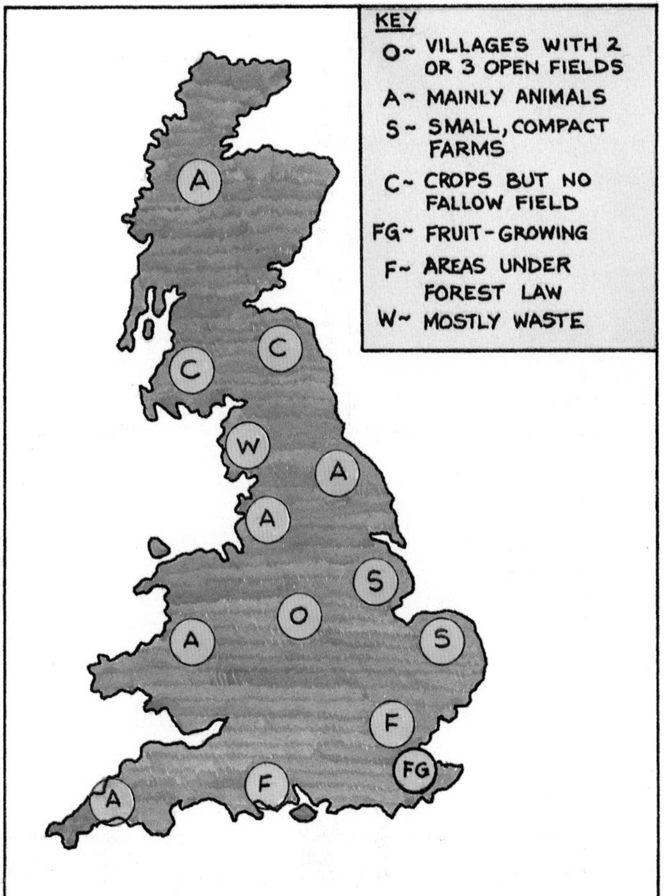

C People farmed differently in different areas. Some areas did not have open fields.

Different sources provide different information. This is not only true of written sources. It is also true of pictures. Some give a different impression to others.

1 In groups, copy this grid onto a sheet of paper.

Item	Made of?	Where from?
Plough Cheese	Wood Goat's Milk	Woodland Wasteland

In the first column, write down as many things as you can which the villagers needed. In the second column, write down what it was made from. Finally, note down which part of the village was used to make it. Two examples have been done for you.

2 a) Write down words to describe the scene and people in source A.
b) Write down words to describe the scene and people in source B.
c) What different impressions of life at this time do they give?
d) Neither picture was painted by an English person. Does this mean they tell us nothing about life in medieval England? Explain your answer.

A The few medieval cottages which have survived did not belong to villeins. This one in Shropshire is a cruck cottage, named after the two curved planks. The poorest cottages were just mud and stone.

LIFE IN THE VILLAGE

The medieval village was very different from a modern one. Few villages had more than 25 families – probably fewer people than in your year group at school. There were no roads leading to it, only muddy trackways.

A villein's home was pretty dingy by our standards. Many were just one-room huts, perhaps 6 metres by 4.5 metres. The walls were made of woven branches called wattle. This was covered with daub – a mixture of clay, dung and straw. Animal hair was used to bind it together.

There were holes for windows and a hole for the door. The floor was just the earth on which the house was built. A fire stood on a lump of stone in the centre of the room. Often there was no chimney. So smoke just curled round the room.

These poor cottages disappeared centuries ago. Each probably only lasted for about 20 years. They had no taps. Water came from a nearby stream. A pit in the garden did for a toilet.

There was hardly anything inside this home: a few farming tools, cooking pots and bowls and perhaps a table and some stools. Better-off peasants might have a spare pair of clothes. Many did not. They might sleep on bags of straw in the same clothes they wore by day. But most pictures of the time show people sleeping naked.

At night-time, the villeins shared their floor with the animals. Sleep, smoke and animals' breath all went together – along with the smell of rotting food and manure.

The animals were the family's most valuable possession. The animals' fleas, of course, were not. But the hut was ideal for fleas to breed.

That goes for lice, too. People could clean their hair with oatmeal, if they could spare it. Often, they did not bother. As people sat gossiping in the evening, they picked the lice from each other's hair. (They cleaned their teeth, if at all, with hazel twigs.)

In the 12th century, life was not much better for a freeman, such as the village priest or the blacksmith. True, their houses were bigger and more sturdy, and they had more possessions. But the glassless windows and the toilet were no different.

However, the freeman did have advantages over the villein. He was at least free to come and go from the village. The villein had to ask his lord if he wanted to travel.

B A village scene from the Middle Ages.

The freeman did not have to work on the lord's land, either. The villein did, every week. He also worked there on 'boon-days' – busy times, such as harvest.

There were about 5,000 slaves in England when William I arrived. The Normans abolished slavery. However, in most respects, the villeins were little better off. And, just like slaves, they could be bought and sold.

C A scene from family life.

Countrywomen's Lives

Married women led lives which were probably harder than the men's. They were expected to help their husbands in the farming work. On top of that, they cleaned the house, cooked and made clothes and brought up the children. A woman might walk up to 32 km (20 miles) just doing a day's spinning.

D Part of *The Servant Girl's Holiday*, a poem of the late Middle Ages.

I've waited longing for today:
Spindle, bobbin, and spool, away!
In joy and bliss I'm off to play
　Upon this high holiday.

The dirt upon the floor's unswept,
The fireplace isn't cleaned and kept,
I haven't cut the rushes yet
　Upon this high holiday.

Now midday has almost come,
And all my chores are still not done:
I'll clean my shoes till they become
　Bright for a high holiday.

E From a German poem, *Helmbrecht*. A man is trying to persuade his sister Gotelinde to choose a rich husband.

You will never be more wretched than if you marry a peasant. You will be forced to spin, to scour the flax, to combe the hemp, wash and wring clothes, dig up the beets.

F *Piers Plowman* by William Langland, written in about 1370.

Pitiful is it to read the cottage woman's woe,
Aye and many another that puts a good face on it,
Ashamed to beg, ashamed to let the neighbours know
All that they need, noontide and evening.
Many the children, and nothing but a man's hands
To clothe and feed them; and few pennies come in,
And many mouths to eat the pennies up,
Bread and thin ale are for them a banquet.

Medieval manuscripts were mostly written by men. They tell us little about women's lives. Yet women played an important role in village life. Sources sometimes have gaps which historians try to fill.

1 a) List a few of the things which your house has which a villein's did not have, such as glass windows. Only compare the buildings.
b) For each thing, suggest how the villein's life was affected by not having it.
c) As the poorest homes have disappeared, how do you think we know what they were like? (More than one answer.)

2 a) *In detail*, explain what you can learn from the sources about women's lives.
b) Which jobs are women doing in source B?
c) Why was each of these jobs important?
d) What do you think a poor woman's main problems were? Write down at least three and put them in order of importance.

3 THE CHURCH

A Above: a stone tenth-century church in Wiltshire. Many Saxon churches were built in wood.

B The Normans introduced new styles of building.

England had had links with Europe long before 1066. It was part of Christendom. This means it was one of the many Christian countries. There was only one Christian Church in the Middle Ages – the Catholic Church. Its leader was the Pope, who lived in Rome. On religious matters, his word was law.

Of course, few people ever met him. When life was hard, villagers went to see their priest. He comforted them. He heard their sins and forgave them.

The church was the very centre of village life. It was the villagers' meeting-place. They swapped news after the service; they played sports in the churchyard; they danced there. Where would they have been without their church?

Its bells told people the time. The bells were even rung to tell people when to plant their peas and beans! And, without the Church, there would have been few holidays.

The Church's holy days became holidays, which is where the word comes from. So there was a week off at Christmas, Easter and Whitsun. Saints' days provided many other days off work.

So it is not surprising that the parish priest was the second most important person in the village. Yet he wasn't always well-educated. In fact, some could not read or write.

Much of the priest's time was spent farming. His own land was called the glebe. It was his main source of income. He earned more money from fees for marriages, funerals and so on.

But most of his income came from the tithe. This was a tax which everyone had to give the church. It was one tenth of all their animals and crops. The priest gave some to the poor. The rest was stored in the tithe barn nearby – until he was ready to sell or eat it.

There were services every day but few people went, except on Sundays. Everyone was too busy farming. In any case, the services meant little to the villagers. The language used was Latin. Villeins and their families did not speak it. Even the priest himself often did not understand it.

But everyone could understand pictures of heaven and hell. So there were pictures in stained glass and paintings on the walls. The first puppet shows were in churches, to help people understand the Bible.

The priest mattered, above all, because he offered something no one else could – the chance to go to heaven. The priest was always there to hear people's problems. He would tell them to live a good life. A good life, he said, was rewarded in heaven. It made sense. After all, that is what the pictures showed. And it didn't seem to be rewarded on earth.

C Medieval people believed in miracles. Gerald of Wales wrote about this one in his *Journey Through Wales* in the late 12th century.

A poor woman used to visit the shrine [of St Edmund], apparently to pray. She came not to give, but to take away. It was her habit to steal the gold and silver offered by others. The way she took it was extremely clever.

She would kiss it, suck it into her lips as she did so, and then carry it away hidden in her mouth. One day as she was actually doing this, her lips and tongue stuck fast to the altar.

She was caught in the act by God's intervention, and she spat out the piece of silver which she had in her mouth. A great crowd of people came running to gape at this. There she remained, fixed, for most of the day, so the miracle was clear for all to see and there could be no doubt about it in anyone's mind.

D Gerald also wrote this account:

A man of these parts, Roger Bechet, owed ten stone of wool to [another man]. Having no more than this, he sent the tenth stone to the church of Caereu (as a tithe), and the remaining nine to his creditor. He begged him to have patience for he would soon make up [the missing stone].

His creditor weighed it and found the weight to be ten stone; and though he weighed it again and again, he always found the full amount of ten stone. So he told Roger that he had received the full amount. The wool had multiplied by a miracle. As a result, many people in those parts have become willing to pay their tithes.

Sometimes, earlier writers have made up details. Or they have believed what others have told them. Historians have to judge what is true and what is not.

1 a) How are sources A and B different?
b) Why would the English have been impressed by the Norman church?

2 a) In source E, what is the attitude of the Lollards to the statue?
b) What is the attitude of the writer to the Lollards? Explain how you know.

3 a) Gerald believed in miracles. Does that mean the stories are true? Give reasons.
b) Think carefully. How would a villager have decided if the stories were true or false?
c) What do you (i) believe and (ii) not believe about the stories? Give your reasons.
d) Why would priests want people to believe these stories? (Two different reasons.)
e) Even if the stories are not true, what can a historian learn from them?

Lollards

Catholics had very clear religious beliefs, such as believing in miracles. People who disagreed with them were called heretics. Some were punished by being burned to death. One 14th-century critic was John Wycliffe.

Wycliffe had two main criticisms. First, he said that some priests were not fit to do the job. Second, he complained that ordinary people could not understand the Bible because it was in Latin. So, in 1382, he translated it into English.

Wycliffe's followers travelled the country, spreading his views. Their opponents said they mumbled and nicknamed them 'Lollards'.

E Lollards also objected to people praying to statues. Henry Knighton, a monk, wrote this story in about 1363.

Richard the priest and William Smith wanted a meal of herbs. They had the herbs but no fire. One peered into a corner of the chapel and saw an old image (statue) made in honour of St Catherine.

'Look, dearly beloved brother,' said he, 'God has given us kindling to cook our meal. This will make a saintly fire.'

So one took the axe and the other took the image, saying, 'Let's test if it's really a saint. If it bleeds when we knock the head off we'll have to adore it. If not, it can feed our fire and cook our vegetables.'

When they came out they could not hide their shame, but gave themselves away to their cost by boasting about it as funny.

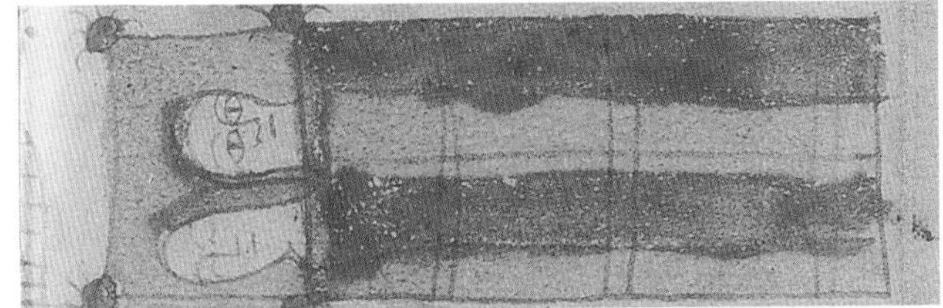

F Everyone was aware of death. These medieval drawings show (from top to bottom) dead children, a dead mother with her newborn child, and even dead cattle.

MONKS AND NUNS

Kings, too, wanted to show their love of God. One way of doing this was to found a monastery. Soon after William I became king, he built one at Battle. It stood on the hill where he had beaten Harold.

By 1250 there were nearly 500 monasteries in the country. During the Middle Ages, many thousands of men and women went to live in them as monks and nuns. (We talk now of nuns living in a nunnery but the word was not used in the Middle Ages.)

These people had decided to devote their lives to God. The life was a strict one. They made three solemn vows: they could not marry; they could not own any possessions; and they had to do whatever the abbot or abbess (chief monk or nun) told them. They could not leave the monastery without permission.

A Young men and women had their hair cut before becoming a monk or nun.

There were different orders of monks. Each dressed in its own way. Each followed different rules. The monks in England in 1066 were all followers of St Benedict. They wore black cloaks, called habits. Their days were spent in work, study and prayer.

However, as time passed, their monasteries grew rich. The monks lived in greater luxury. A few ignored the rules about having no possessions. They ate and drank well. Servants did the work for them.

Over in France, a monk called Bernard did not approve. His monks still lived a strict, hard-working life. They were the Cistercian monks. But people often called them *white monks* because they wore white cloaks. In 1131, a group of them came to England. Here, they built new monasteries in lonely areas.

Beautiful new buildings were put up in Yorkshire. Others were built in remote parts of Scotland and Wales. Here, the monks spent much of their time breeding sheep. Ordinary people, called lay brothers, helped them.

Some women, too, wanted to devote their lives to God. However, there were other reasons why a woman might become a nun. Nobles often sent a daughter to a nunnery, especially if they could not find her a husband.

Older women sometimes preferred being a nun to getting married. It was the only real career open to a medieval woman. Others became nuns after their husbands died. Few nunneries were well-off; they were grateful for the money a widow would give them.

As a result, it grew difficult to keep to all the strict rules. By the 15th century, some nuns kept pet dogs in their nunneries. They turned up late to services and sometimes slept right through them. Others didn't turn up at all, perhaps because they had had too much to drink the night before.

Some monks were no better. The Cistercian monks had grown rich through sheep farming. It had become easier to pay lay brothers to do the work for them.

B A 14-century picture showing nuns in the refectory. One nun reads from a holy book. The others eat silently.

C One important job was done by monks throughout the Middle Ages. They copied books. Without them we would know far less of the history of this period. They also illuminated them with coloured inks. The pictures tell us a lot about life at the time. This source is from a life of the French King, Louis IX (about 1375). At the bottom left he is shown collecting up holy relics (saints' bones).

1 a) How did the lives of these people change during the Middle Ages: (i) Benedictine monks; (ii) Cistercian monks; (iii) nuns; (iv) friars?
b) What do you notice about your answers?
c) Does this prove that all monks forgot their vows? Explain your answer.

2 Please work in pairs.
a) Look at source C. Two of the scenes show King Louis with monks. What is happening in these scenes?
b) How can you tell that he was a holy person from the way he is drawn?
c) How can you tell that he was very religious from his actions in the middle picture on the right?

Life in a monastery changed a great deal between 1066 and 1500. *Many* of the later monks and nuns ignored their vows. For instance, they wore the finest gold crosses and rings. However, this does not mean that *every* monk and nun behaved like this.

The Friars

In the 13th century, a new group of people arrived in England. These were the Franciscan friars. They were named after Francis, the man who started them. Friars, too, promised to stay poor and devote their lives to God. However, they did not go to live in monasteries.

Friars spent their time travelling around, helping the poor and sick. They owned nothing of their own. They begged for food; they got shelter where they could. People were impressed by their love and care.

But, as time passed, the friars were often given gifts, just as the monks had been. In time, they built fine friaries, rather like the monasteries. Some grew rich and ignored their vows. By 1381, there was a saying, 'This is a friar, and therefore a liar.'

D One friar that most people know – Friar Tuck, the greedy friar of the Robin Hood stories. This actor appeared in a television series, *Robin of Sherwood*.

3 a) Look at source D. Is this a primary or secondary source? Explain how you decided.
b) Friar Tuck is a character in a story. How can fiction help historians understand the past?
c) Friar Tuck was supposed to be living in England during Richard I's reign. Why can't this be true?
d) Does this mean that the Robin Hood stories are of no use to historians?

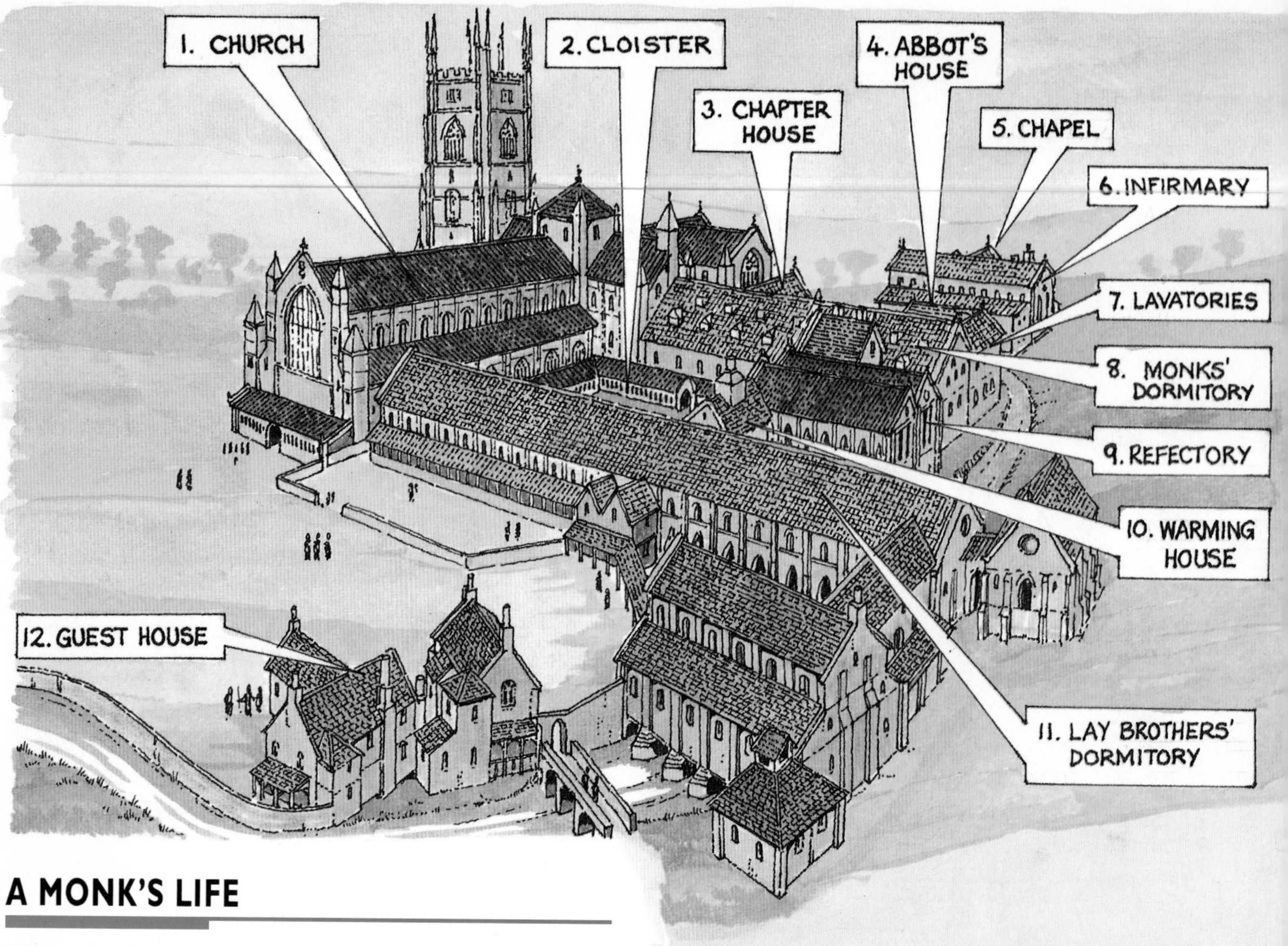

1. CHURCH
2. CLOISTER
3. CHAPTER HOUSE
4. ABBOT'S HOUSE
5. CHAPEL
6. INFIRMARY
7. LAVATORIES
8. MONKS' DORMITORY
9. REFECTORY
10. WARMING HOUSE
11. LAY BROTHERS' DORMITORY
12. GUEST HOUSE

A MONK'S LIFE

When the Domesday Book was written, monasteries had more land than anyone else. They even had more than the King. They added to this land during the Middle Ages. It is hard for us nowadays to imagine just how powerful this made them.

However, we can imagine what the monks' lives were like. There is plenty of written evidence about this. And archaeologists have studied the remains of monastery buildings.

This picture shows what Fountains Abbey in Yorkshire looked like during the Middle Ages. It was owned by Cistercian monks. They made it one of the richest monasteries in the land. Today, only ruins remain.

These sources give us information about life in a monastery. Sources A and B describe Cistercian monks; sources C and E describe Benedictine monks. Different orders of monks lived in different ways.

A Abbot Ailred described life at Rievaulx Abbey in 1135.

Our food is scanty, our garments are rough; our drink is from the stream. Under our tired limbs there is but a hard mat; when sleep is sweetest we must rise at a bell's bidding. There is no moment for idleness.

Everywhere peace, and a marvellous freedom from the tumult of the world, such unity is there among the brethren that each thing seems to belong to all, and all to each.

B But not everyone found the life easy to cope with:

I am tormented and crushed down by the length of the vigils [night prayers]. I often [yield] to the manual labour. The rough clothing cuts through my skin. More than this, my will is always hankering after other things. It longs for the delights of the world and sighs for its pleasures.

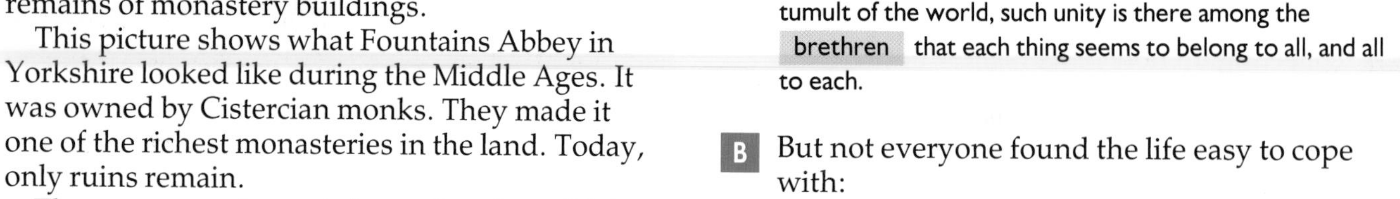

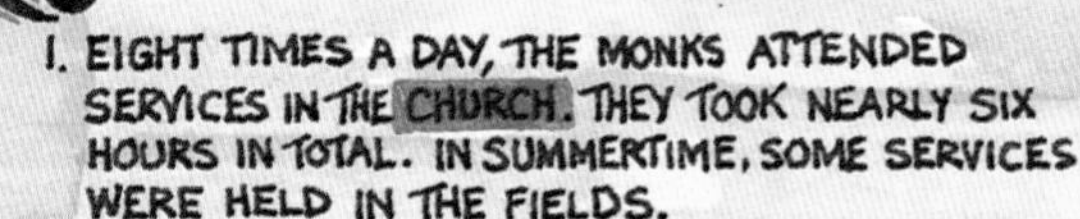

1. EIGHT TIMES A DAY, THE MONKS ATTENDED SERVICES IN THE **CHURCH**. THEY TOOK NEARLY SIX HOURS IN TOTAL. IN SUMMERTIME, SOME SERVICES WERE HELD IN THE FIELDS.
2. MONKS READ OR WALKED IN THE **CLOISTER**. IT WAS A COVERED WALK ROUND AN OPEN GRASSY SQUARE.
3. ALL THE MONKS MET EVERY MORNING IN THE **CHAPTER HOUSE**. RULES WERE READ. PUNISHMENTS WERE GIVEN OUT. WORK WAS DISCUSSED.
4. THE **ABBOT** HAD HIS OWN PRIVATE ROOMS.
5. A SEPARATE **CHAPEL** FOR SICK MONKS STOPPED DISEASES FROM SPREADING.
6. THE **INFIRMARY** WAS FOR SICK MONKS. THE MONASTERY GREW ITS OWN HERBS. OUTSIDERS PAID MONKS FOR MEDICAL ADVICE.
7. THE **LAVATORIES** DRAINED STRAIGHT INTO THE STREAM.
8. THE **MONKS' DORMITORY** ORIGINALLY HAD NO PARTITIONS BETWEEN THE BEDS.
9. IN THE **REFECTORY** (DINING-ROOM), THE MONKS ATE IN SILENCE. THERE WAS ONE MEAL A DAY FROM SEPTEMBER TO EASTER, EXCEPT ON SUNDAYS. MEAT WAS NOT ALLOWED ORIGINALLY.
10. THE **WARMING HOUSE** WAS WHERE MONKS KEPT WARM ON A WINTER'S DAY. MONKS COULD SPEAK TO GUESTS HERE.
11. THE **LAY BROTHERS' DORMITORY** HOUSED THE LAY BROTHERS, POOR MEN WHO COULD NOT READ. THEY DID NOT ATTEND EVERY SERVICE. THEY ALSO ATE IN A SEPARATE REFECTORY.
12. ALL MONASTERIES HAD A **GUEST HOUSE**. ANYONE COULD STAY THERE. POOR TRAVELLERS PAID WITH A PRAYER.

SHEEP PROVIDED WOOL FOR MONKS' HABITS. THE REST WAS SOLD. THE MONASTERY GREW RICH FROM SHEEP-FARMING.

C From a 10th-century rule-book for monasteries.

On Saturdays the brethren shall wash their feet, for which purpose each shall have a suitable basin. Having washed their feet, those who need to shall wash their shoes also.

D *The Times* (1987) gave news of archaeologists' discoveries.

Excavations into a graveyard are providing a glimpse of monastic life in twelfth-century Britain. The archaeologists have discovered that a life of prayer could be hard for the [monks].

One of the skeletons found showed signs of arthritis in the knee. Mr Currie, in charge of the dig, [said this was] 'hardly surprising for a monk who spends most of his life in a cold church on his knees.'

E From the 11th-century rule-book at Canterbury: *The Monastic Constitutions of Lanfranc*.

He who is to be punished shall be beaten with a single stout rod while he lies in his shift on the ground, or with a bundle of finer rods while he sits with his back bare. While he is being beaten all the brethren should bow down with compassion for him. No one should speak.

1 You are a monk at Fountains Abbey. Describe in detail one day in your life. You could do this in one of these ways:

- a diary entry
- a written description
- a letter to another monk
- mime
- a tape-recording
- a picture-strip

Your account *must* use some information from the sources. You may add drawings to a written account, if you wish. If you do, label them carefully.

4 A KING AND AN ARCHBISHOP

1000 1100 1200 1300 1400 1500

The Church was very powerful in the Middle Ages. So was the monarch. From time to time, a quarrel between them was bound to happen. The most famous quarrel happened in the late 12th century between a king and an archbishop.

The king was Henry II, who became king in 1154. William I, his great-grandfather, had ruled Normandy and England. Henry II also ruled more than half of France. In fact, he ruled more of France than the King of France himself.

Henry II was just 21 when he became king. He had amazing energy. He exhausted officials who worked for him. He even dictated letters to his secretary during prayers in church.

Spending a great deal of time in France created a problem. Someone had to control England while he was away. He needed someone whom he could trust – and someone who was clever. He chose Thomas Becket.

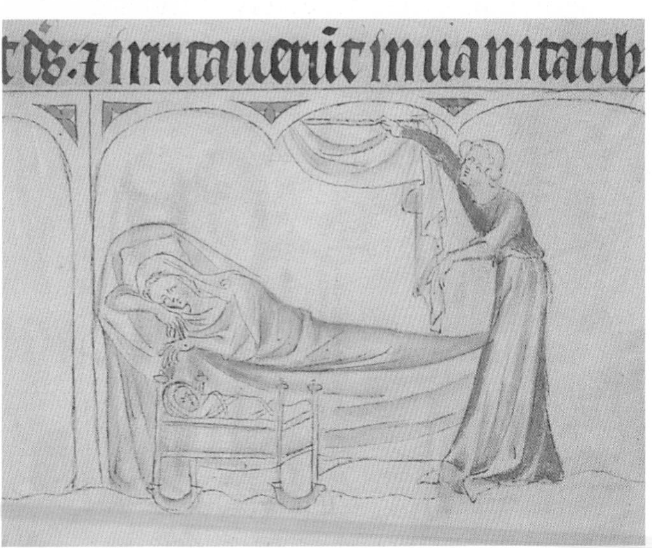

A The birth of Thomas Becket from *Queen Mary's Psalter* (Book of Psalms), early 14th century.

Thomas was born in 1118. His father was a Norman merchant who lived in London. Early on, Thomas chose a career in the Church. All his life, people called him Thomas. The name *Becket* may have meant *beaky*. He had a nose hooked like an eagle's.

Thomas became Henry II's Chancellor. By all accounts, he was good at the job. It was Thomas who helped Henry II bring the barons under control. He even fought for Henry. He led an army in France and won even more land for his king.

Thomas soon became the second most important man in England. He owned castles and manors. When people visited, he offered them the best food, served on fine gold plate. The food was better than that served by the King. There was more gold, too. But, despite all his wealth, Thomas was totally loyal to Henry.

In 1162, the Archbishop of Canterbury died. This gave Henry the chance he had been waiting for. He had been trying to improve law and order in his lands. He had partly succeeded. But one thing still stood in his way.

The Church still had its own courts. Any priest or monk could choose to be tried by a Church court, not by the King's court. They nearly always did. The King's courts gave stiffer sentences.

B A mosaic of Thomas from a cathedral in Sicily, founded by Henry II's daughter. It was made in about 1190 for people who had known Thomas.

1 a) Look at source A. Do you think this is an accurate picture? Give reasons.
b) Look at source B. Why might this picture be more accurate than source A?
c) Even if source A is not accurate, what can a historian learn from it?

A convicted thief might have his or her eyes put out in a royal court. A Church court might just send them on a pilgrimage . A royal court would hang a murderer. The worst that happened in a Church court was that they were excommunicated .

Henry II wanted an Archbishop of Canterbury who would end all this. He wanted an Archbishop who would do what he was told. What he wanted, he decided, was Thomas as Archbishop of Canterbury.

Thomas did not want the job. 'Our friendship,' he warned the King, 'will turn to hate.' The monks did not want Thomas, either. They knew he lived in luxury. He seemed completely the wrong person for the job. But Henry got his way. In 1162, Thomas became Archbishop of Canterbury.

Overnight, he became a changed man. The poor now got the rich food. He lived on bread and water. There were fine sheets on his bed. But he often slept on the floor.

In 1164, Henry made a law which said that anyone found guilty in a Church court would be punished in the King's court. Thomas refused to agree and the quarrel grew bitter. That same year, knowing he was in danger, Thomas fled abroad.

C John of Salisbury supported Thomas. John had gone into exile in France in October 1163. That month, he wrote from France to Thomas who was still in England. This is part of the letter.

Count Philip was eager to learn from me the state of things in England. He asked many questions about the King and the nobles. He sympathises with your troubles, and promises his help. When you need ships, he will supply them.

After having settled myself in my lodgings, I went and laid your business before the [French] King: he expresses great sympathy in your sufferings and promises you help.

He said he had already written to the Pope in your favour. If necessary, [he] will write again, or see the Pope in person. The French are much afraid of our King Henry, and hate him most intensely, but this between ourselves.

Rome [where the Pope lived] was never proof against bribes, and none of them would like to offend your King. Now what can we do, needy as we are, against such powerful enemies? We have only words to offer, and the Italians will not listen to them.

Their respect for the King and his messengers will lead them to take a large sum from them rather than a small sum from us.

In 1170, Henry and Thomas patched up their quarrel. Thomas returned to Canterbury. But, while he had been away, the King had asked the Archbishop of York to crown his son. Two bishops helped him.

This job was usually done by the Archbishop of Canterbury. So Thomas asked the Pope to punish the other archbishop. He also excommunicated the bishops. It was a very serious punishment. It meant that they could not hope to go to heaven when they died. It also meant that the quarrel with the King was not over.

D Thomas arrived back in England in 1170. This picture illustrated a life story of Thomas, produced in about 1235.

A timeline is a way of showing events in chronological order. When drawing a timeline, all intervals must be of equal size. The dates should be written on one side of the line. The events are recorded on the other side.

2 Draw a timeline of the 12th century to show events in this chapter. Use one centimetre for each decade (ten years). Include these events: (a) the birth of Thomas: (b) Henry II becomes King; (c) Thomas becomes Archbishop; (d) Thomas flees to France; (e) Thomas returns to Canterbury.

3 Read source C.
a) Which people offer to help Thomas?
b) According to John, what is Thomas trying to do?
c) Is he likely to succeed? Give a reason.
d) What do you think Henry would feel, if he had read this letter?

4 a) Work in pairs. One of you is the King; one is Thomas. Decide what you would do at this point in the quarrel.
b) When you have decided, the 'King' should tell 'Thomas' what he will do next. 'Thomas' should reply, as planned.
c) How did this add to your understanding of the quarrel?

DEATH AT CANTERBURY

Henry was in France when he heard what Thomas had done. He was very angry. Henry's temper was well-known. (Bad tempers ran in his family.) Sometimes, he would roll on the floor and gnaw the rushes.

'Is there no one,' Henry cried, 'who will rid me of this troublesome priest?'

Four knights overheard this remark. They decided to do what Henry wanted. They quickly set sail for England. Once they landed, they rode straight for Canterbury. Three more knights were sent to stop them, but it was too late.

Thomas was warned that they were coming. That Christmas Day, he told people that an earlier archbishop was already a **martyr**. Soon, he said, there might be a second.

At about five o'clock on 29 December 1170, the knights reached the cathedral. Thomas was inside. What happened next is described and shown in primary sources. Check carefully to see how they agree and how they disagree.

Historians try to find out people's motives, such as why the knights acted as they did. We also need to decide the causes of events. Sources A, B and C are primary sources for St Thomas's death. We need to compare these sources to find out why Thomas was killed.

C This is the earliest picture of the event, made in about 1180. It shows four separate events, starting with the news of the knights' arrival (top left).

D (Bottom right) The burial of the Archbishop. This picture was made within 50 years of his death.

A Edward Grim was a monk at Canterbury. He was an eye-witness to the events. He wrote this account between 1175 and 1177.

When the monks entered the church, already the four knights followed behind with rapid strides. With them was a subdeacon, armed with malice like their own, Hugh . . .

The monks hastened to protect their shepherd from the slaughter by bolting the doors of the church. But [Becket] ordered the church doors to be thrown open, saying, 'It is not right to make the house of prayer into a fortress.'

The knights called out, 'Where is Thomas Becket, **traitor** to the King and country? Where is the Archbishop?'

In a clear voice [he] answered, 'I am here, no traitor to the King, but a priest. Why do you seek me?' He added, 'So I am ready to suffer in His name. Far be it for me to flee from your swords, or to depart from justice.'

'Forgive those whom you have excommunicated.'

He answered: 'I will not.'

'Then you shall die,' they cried, 'and receive what you deserve.'

'I am ready,' he said, 'to die for my Lord, so that the Church can obtain freedom and peace. But I forbid you to hurt my people.'

Then they tried to pull and drag him so that they could kill him outside the church, or carry him away as a prisoner, as they afterwards confessed. But he could not be forced away from the pillar.

One of them pressed on him and clung to him more closely. [Becket] pushed him off, saying, 'Do not touch me, Reginald. You owe me loyalty. You and your accomplices are acting like madmen.'

Then the martyr bowed his neck as if praying and lifted up his hands in prayer.

He had hardly spoken when the wicked knight, afraid that Thomas might be rescued and escape, suddenly leapt upon him and wounded him in the head, cutting the top. With the same blow, he almost cut off my arm. For, when the others fled, [I] stuck close to the Archbishop and held him in [my] arms till one was almost severed.

Then he received a second blow on the head but still stood firm. At the third blow he fell on his knees and elbows, offering himself as a sacrifice. He said in a low voice, 'For the name of Jesus and the protection of the Church, I am ready to die.'

Then the third knight inflicted a terrible wound as he lay there. By this stroke, the sword was broken against the pavement. The top was cut off his head so that the blood stained the cathedral floor. The fourth knight prevented anyone from interfering.

The fifth man put his foot on the neck of the holy priest and martyr and scattered his brains and blood over the pavement, calling out, 'Let us away, knights. He will rise no more.'

B William fitzStephen was another eye-witness. He wrote *Life of St Thomas Becket* in the 1170s.

Not afraid to die for the freedom and the cause of Christ's Church, he told [the monks] to depart, so that they might not stop his sufferings. He had foretold these and now saw they were about to occur.

He was proceeding towards the altar when Reginald fitzUrse appeared, dressed in suit of mail and with drawn sword, shouting, 'Hither now to me, King's men!' He was joined by three comrades, also dressed in full armour, and a great many others, also armed.

The monks wished to close and bolt the doors of the church. But the good Archbishop forbade the monks to close the door, saying, 'Far be it from us to turn the church of God into a fortress. God's will be done.'

[At this point,] John of Salisbury and his other [priests] fled – all except Robert the canon, William fitzStephen and Edward Grim. Had he wished, the Archbishop might easily have saved himself by flight.

The executioners came running through the open door. Someone shouted, 'Where is the traitor?' The Archbishop made no reply.

Someone else said, 'Where is the Archbishop?' He answered, 'Here am I, no traitor, but a priest of God. I marvel that you have entered the church in such clothes. What do you want with me?'

One cut-throat replied, 'Your death.'

'I submit to death,' replied the Archbishop, 'in the name of the Lord. Far be it from me to flee from your swords. But I forbid you to touch any of these servants of mine.'

One struck him with the flat of the sword between the shoulders, saying, 'Fly, you are a dead man.' But the Archbishop stood unmoved, offering his neck.

Some of the enemy cried, 'You are our prisoner, come with us.' They would have dragged him out of the church, but for fear that the people might rescue him from their clutches. The Archbishop answered, 'Here you shall do your will and obey your orders.'

Master Edward Grim, putting up his arm, received the first stroke aimed by William de Traci at the Archbishop's head. The Archbishop was wounded in the head by the same stroke.

The Archbishop knelt down. A second stroke was dealt him on the head, at which he fell flat on his face. While he lay there, Richard Brito hit him with such force that the sword was broken against his head and the pavement of the church. 'Take that,' he said, 'for love of my lord William, the King's brother.'

The saintly Archbishop received four wounds in all, all in the head. The whole crown of his head was lopped off. It was obvious that he did not struggle against death.

Hugh of Horsea put his foot on the neck of the fallen martyr and extracted the blood and brains from the hollow of his severed crown with the point of his sword.

As the body lay there, the townsfolk came in. Some brought bottles and took away some blood. Others tore off bits of Thomas's clothing and dipped them in his blood. Within hours, people were claiming miracles.

The Pope quickly made Thomas a saint. People came from all over Europe to pray at his **shrine**. Henry II asked the Pope's forgiveness. The King returned to England and walked barefoot to St Thomas's tomb. Monks whipped him as he lay there.

The pilgrims left gifts on the shrine. It was a way of saying thanks for miracles which St Thomas had brought about. By the 15th century, the shrine was covered with sheets of gold. Diamonds and rubies clustered upon it.

It stayed there until the 16th century. Then, Henry VIII closed down the monasteries and took the valuables away. It took 21 carts to remove all the treasure.

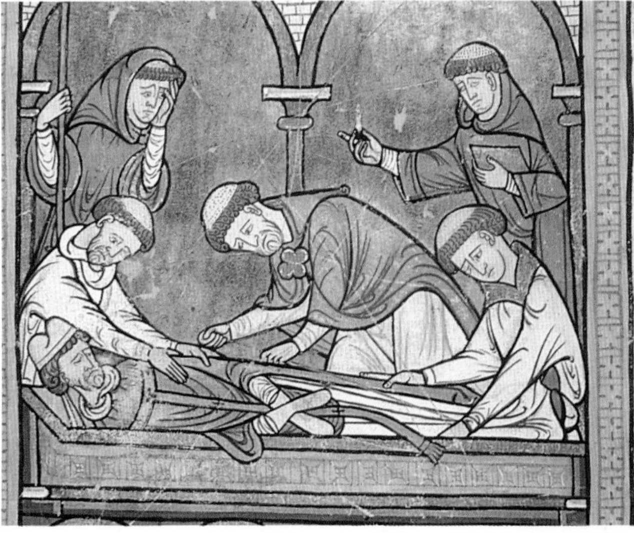

1 a) What part did Henry play in Thomas's death?
b) What do you think the knights' motives were?
c) How can you tell that Henry did not intend them to do this?
d) Did Thomas do anything to avoid his death? Explain your answer.
e) Did he do anything to cause his death? Explain carefully.

2 a) Read sources A and B. What extra information does source B provide?
b) How do the two sources disagree about who stayed with Thomas?
c) If source A is correct, where did the author of source B get his information? Explain your answer.
d) Write down two other details on which these two sources disagree.
e) For each source, (A, B and C) give a mark out of ten to show how reliable you think it is.
f) What questions did you ask yourself about these sources when you answered question (e)?

5 KING JOHN'S GREAT CHARTER

1000 1100 1200 1300 1400 1500

Henry II had a quick temper. His son John was just as bad. But the real problem was that people did not really trust John. Soon after he became king, John captured his nephew Arthur. He was put in prison. Then, the boy disappeared. Many people thought that John had him murdered.

Quite soon, John quarrelled with the Pope about who should be Archbishop of Canterbury. As a result, the Pope put the country under an Interdict. This meant that all English churches had to close. Not being able to go to church was a serious matter. It meant people could not confess their sins. People feared this meant they would go to hell.

At one point, the Pope excommunicated the King. The churches were shut for six years before John gave in. He told the Pope that, in future, the Pope would be his overlord. John would be just his humble servant.

But King John's troubles were not over. In 1214, the French army defeated the English. Henry II's great empire was soon lost. All that was left were the Channel Islands and Bordeaux.

This meant many barons lost land they had in France. They were already angry with John because he kept lands which were not his. Also, he put people in prison without trial.

A This statue of King John was made about 20 years after he died. We cannot tell if it is true-to-life.

John's fines annoyed the barons. One baron called Robert gave the King five horses to stop him talking about another man's wife. They also objected to a tax of £2 which the King had demanded in 1214.

B This drawing by Matthew Paris shows people being punished during King John's reign.

During the winter, the barons produced a charter. The barons asked King John to agree to it. In future, they were saying, you must stick to the laws of the country.

King John refused. He would not, he swore, become the barons' slave. But in May 1215, about 500 knights marched on London. They attacked the Tower of London.

On 15 June, King John met the knights at an island in the River Thames called Runnymede. He put his seal on their charter, all 63 clauses of it. This showed he accepted it. But afterwards, one writer said, he threw himself on the ground and gnawed sticks and straws.

John never intended to keep his promise. He contacted the Pope, who said that John was not bound to keep his promise. Soon, fighting broke out. But, while it was still going on, John died.

John left behind one of the great documents of British history. It was written in Latin so they called it 'Magna Carta', Latin for *Great Charter*.

In fact, there was little that was new in it and it only gave rights to free people. Most of the population, of course, were peasants. So it did not apply to them. However, centuries later, everyone would be free and enjoy these rights.

Historians have disagreed about how good or bad King John was. There are two basic views. Some historians saw him as the worst king the country ever had.

John was, they said, wicked and a hopeless king. He treated people cruelly and was unjust. On top of that, he had an awful temper. In the end, these historians say, the barons forced him to agree to Magna Carta. It was what he deserved. He was a really nasty person.

This view was first written down by Matthew Paris and Roger of Wendover. They were monks writing in the 13th century.

Other historians disagree. They say John was a clever ruler who organised the country better than before. He made governments, and monarchs, stronger than ever before.

Two different people may see an event in quite different ways. Early writers about King John were often biased. They gave a one-sided picture of him. Today, some historians look back on his reign and take a different view.

C Winston Churchill: *History of the English-Speaking Peoples* (1956–8).

Normandy finally became French. No English tears need have been shed over this. The separation was as much in the interest of England as of France. It turned [English] thought and energies to its own affairs. However, [this] did not dawn on John's contemporaries, who saw only a humiliating defeat. They blamed King John.

D The *Barnwell Chronicle*, written by a monk in the 13th century.

He was a great Prince certainly but hardly a happy one. He experienced ups and downs of fortune. Ireland, Scotland and Wales all bowed to his nod – which no [earlier kings] had achieved. He would have thought he was as happy and successful as he could have wished, if he had not lost [lands in France] and suffered the Church's curse.

1 Who would be made angry by each of the events below? Choose your answer from this list: the barons; King John; the Pope; ordinary people; the French; criminals. Give reasons for your choices.
a) Land was lost in France.
b) John wanted to choose the new Archbishop.
c) The Pope forced the churches to close.
d) People were put in prison without trial.
e) John was forced to sign Magna Carta.

2 Read this page carefully.
a) Why do you think *monks* disliked John so much?
b) Why must historians treat what these monks said carefully?
c) How do sources C and D agree and disagree?
d) Why do you think writers at the time did not think losing French lands was good?
e) Does this mean that historical events can only be judged later? Explain your answer fully.

6 THE BEGINNING OF PARLIAMENT

1000 1100 1200 1300 1400 1500

John's son, Henry III, did not have a peaceful reign. Henry allowed Frenchmen to come to England. He gave them English lands and titles. Of course, most of the English barons themselves spoke French and had French names. But they looked on these new French immigrants as foreigners.

In the end, the barons revolted. They were led by an earl called Simon de Montfort. This may seem odd – he was French, too! In 1264, Simon beat Henry III in a battle at Lewes in Sussex. Henry was captured.

In 1265, Simon decided to call people together to decide how the country should be ruled. Councils had met before. King John's Councils were usually attended by barons. Sometimes, two knights from each county were there, too.

Simon's Council was different. For the first time, there were also people representing the towns. The two knights from each county were joined by two burgesses to represent each town or city.

Simon himself was killed in battle later that year. But the idea he started has stayed with us ever since. Henry's son, Edward I, continued to call Councils. Sometimes, he, too, included two citizens from each town.

Edward knew that these towns were growing rich. Some of their merchants were as rich as some nobles. He could not afford to ignore them if he needed more taxes.

During the 13th century, people chose a new name for these Councils. They called them *Parliaments*, from the French word *parler*, meaning *to talk*. A full Parliament included barons and clergy, knights and burgesses. The last two groups were elected, rather like MPs are today.

These Parliaments met at Westminster. They only came together when the King wanted them to meet. There were 52 meetings during the 35 years of Edward I's reign. And they often met for one simple reason: the King needed money – and he wanted Parliament to agree to taxes.

The burgesses were not all that keen on going. For many of them, it was a long journey. Then, when they arrived, the barons looked down on them. They were, the barons thought, just jumped-up merchants, not great landowners like themselves.

So the burgesses began to meet separately, along with the knights. That way, they could say what they wanted. The wealthy barons could not force them to do what they did not wish.

By the end of the 14th century, they were meeting in the abbey at Westminster. It was their first home – the first House of Commons. They were called *commons* because they were ordinary people, not nobles.

A Sir Thomas Hungerford was one of the first Speakers of the House of Commons. This means he had to tell the King the views of the knights and burgesses.

B Edward I at a meeting of Parliament. This secondary source was drawn in the 16th century. The King's ministers are seated on the woolsacks in the centre. Wool made the country rich. The men in blue are bishops.

C This summons for a Parliament was issued by King Edward I in 1304. Amongst other things, he wanted to discuss Scotland.

Because of certain matters that especially concern our realm of England and the settlement of our land of Scotland, and also various other business to be discussed; we wish to hold a Parliament on the 16th of February next at Westminster, with the nobles and important people of the Kingdom.

The **sheriffs** are to choose without delay from each county two knights, and from any city in the county two citizens, and from any borough two burgesses. And the sheriffs are to cause them to come to us at the aforesaid time and place.

The barons carried on meeting with the bishops and abbots. These were the great lords of the land. So, together, they were known as 'The House of Lords'.

Much the same was happening in Scotland. The King's council was first called a 'Parliament' in 1293. The first burgesses attended in 1326. They, too, were called together because the King needed money. Edward I held his first Parliament in Ireland in 1297.

Today, Britain is actually ruled by the House of Lords and the House of Commons. Unlike in Edward I's time, the real decisions are now made in the House of Commons. Together, these two groups make the laws we have to live by.

All members of the modern House of Commons are chosen in an election. Everyone over 18 can vote to choose the Members of Parliament who will represent them.

1 Explain the meaning of each of these words: burgess; Parliament; House of Commons; House of Lords.

2 a) In what ways is the modern Parliament similar to that of the Middle Ages?
b) In what ways is it different?

3 You need to watch a short video of a meeting of the House of Lords.
a) How do the scenes you see differ from the picture above?
b) In what ways are the scenes the same?
c) People in the Middle Ages could not watch Parliament on TV. Why not?
d) You *can* watch Parliament on TV. Is this progress? Explain your answer.
e) The members of the House of Lords are still not elected. Does this mean the House of Lords has not progressed? Give reasons.

7 TOWN LIFE

A medieval street scene – or is it? See question 1.

There were just six large towns when William I had the Domesday Book made. The others had fewer then 4,000 people living in them. They were no bigger than a modern village.

Many started as market-places. They were places where country people brought spare food to swap. They tended to be at places where people could meet easily, such as a crossroads. Others grew around a river, at a spot where it could easily be crossed.

These towns had to be safe. Merchants would not come unless they felt sure their goods were safe. So the lords built wooden fences or walls around them. At night, the gates were locked to stop foreigners (outsiders) from getting in.

Many towns were owned by the King himself. Others were owned by lords, just as other lords owned manors. In fact, life was similar to village life. Each morning, many townsfolk went out to work on the lord's lands. But there were no villeins in the towns. In towns, everyone was free. Runaway villeins who stayed there for a year and a day became free.

The lord was keen to see his town grow. Merchants paid taxes. They were collected by the sheriff, who usually collected extra money for himself. So naturally, townspeople preferred to collect their own taxes.

They could do this by buying a charter. This was a document which gave townspeople certain rights. One thing the people nearly always wanted was the chance to collect their own taxes. They often asked for their own court to settle legal squabbles.

If possible, they wanted the right to be free. This meant not having to pay taxes to the lord and not having to work on his land. On top of that, they might demand the right to hold a fair or market. They knew that these would make the town richer.

Even so, medieval towns were small, dirty and very smelly places. Most streets were just muddy tracks. Open gutters ran along them and people threw their waste food and sewage into it. You had to watch your head as you passed by! London had twelve carts to collect rubbish by 1400. But most towns left it to dogs, pigs and rats to eat it up.

Parliament passed various laws to clean up towns. They had little effect. Butchers continued to throw animal waste into the street. A dung-heap was a common sight – and smell! Of course, it spread disease. So did the filthy water. As one writer said, water was infected 'with frogges and worms'.

Fire was another risk. Most houses were made of wood, and that included the chimneys. Towns were unsafe for other reasons, too. There were no street lights. So it could be dangerous to travel after dark. There was also the risk of tripping over a stray pig – and of landing up in a dung-heap!

A Richard of Devizes: *Chronicles of the Crusaders*. He describes various towns in 1204.

Bath: Bath is placed in the lowest parts of the valleys, in a sulphury vapour, as if it were at the gates of hell.

Worcester, Chester, Hereford: Do not select your home in the northern cities, nor in Worcester, Chester, Hereford, because of the desperate Welshmen.

York: York is full of Scots, vile and faithless men, or rather rascals.

Ely: The town of Ely is always rotting because of the marshes.

B *The White Book of the City of London* (1419). The following rules were passed to clean up the city.

That the Streets and Lanes shall be cleaned of all obstacles from dung and chips.

That no one shall throw dung into the King's Highway, or before the house of his neighbour.

That each person shall make clean of filth the front of his house under penalty of half a mark.

C A street scene in 14th-century France. The object on the far right is a sugar-loaf.

There is no such thing as a useless source. All sources contain information. This is true even if the author is biased or the artist has not shown things exactly as they are.

1 In pairs, look at the scene on page 34. The artist has drawn a medieval street scene but he has included ten mistakes. Try to find all ten. Write down each one and explain why it is a mistake.

2 a) List the differences between a modern town and a medieval town.
b) Which of your senses (sight, hearing, etc) would *first* notice the difference as you approached a medieval town? Explain your answer carefully.

3 a) Look at source C below. Do you think all streets were like this? Explain your answer.
b) What can a historian learn from this scene?
c) This is a French scene. Does this mean it tells us nothing about medieval England? Give reasons.

4 a) Read source A. Is this writer biased or not? Quote from the source in your answer.
b) How does source B support the text on page 34?

CRAFT WORKERS

There were no factories in the Middle Ages. Craftspeople set up stalls outside their own homes or used their front room. They made goods in full view of the public. Above the stall they hung a sign so everyone could tell what they sold.

In time, these craftspeople organised themselves into **guilds**. There was one guild for each trade. Only skilled workers could join. The guild made sure that their products were good quality and that members charged honest prices.

Each year, the guild chose some of its members as 'searchers'. Their job was to visit traders to make sure the rules were obeyed. They checked scales; they tasted food; they inspected the work.

Members whose work was poor were often fined. The guild could also force them to do the work again. Once in a while, it actually expelled someone. This meant they could no longer trade in the town.

The government did not help the old and sick in those days. So the guild looked after its members when they were sick. They helped the relatives of dead craftspeople. They also gave money to the Church and the town.

The youngest guild members were the apprentices. These were boys or girls, aged about twelve, who wanted to learn a trade. Their parents made an agreement with a master craftsman (or craftswoman) who would teach them. Usually, they paid the master for this.

The working year in York in the 15th century. Guild members could only work during daylight hours. (Working hours were often longer 400 years later.)

The agreement was written down on a piece of paper which was then cut up. One piece was given to each side. If, in the future, there was any argument about it, they simply put the two bits together to prove the agreement had been made.

The apprentice went to live with the master for between 4 and 14 years. The master promised that he or she would teach the young person the trade. They also had to look after the apprentice; food and clothing were provided; and the apprentice was taught how to behave.

In return, the apprentice promised to work hard and not to give away any of the employer's secrets. The young person could not go to an inn. Usually, they were not allowed to get married either.

A A tailor's shop in Italy in the Middle Ages.

When the time was up, the apprentice often went on working for the master. Now the young person received a daily wage, so he or she was called a journeyman (from the word *journée*, meaning 'a day'). Journeymen were free to work for a different master. Earnings were carefully saved up, ready for the day when they could set up their own business.

Before this happened, the guild set a test. Journeymen had to produce a 'masterpiece'. This was one piece of work to show that they were fit to open their own shop. If they passed, they, too, became masters of their craft.

Only guild members could sell inside the town, except on market days. People came from far and wide to sell goods at the market. Even more people, including foreign merchants, turned up for the annual fair. This was usually held after the harvest, when people could afford to buy.

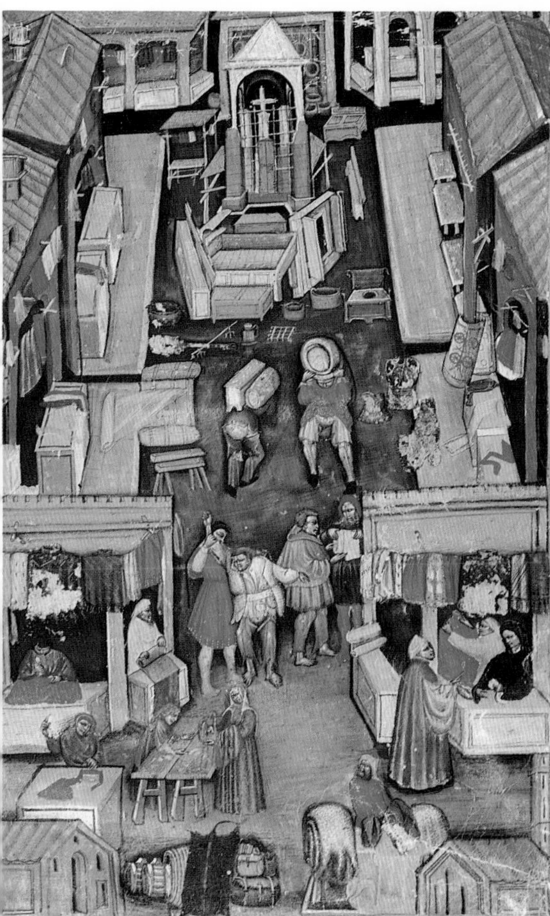

B A covered market in 15th-century France.

Modern shops and medieval ones have the same aim. They sell goods to the public. Shops have, of course, changed a great deal in the last 600 years. This does not mean that every change is for the better.

1 What or who was: (a) a searcher, (b) an apprentice, (c) a journeyman and (d) a masterpiece?

2 a) How do modern shops differ from the shops in sources A and B?
b) What are the advantages of goods actually being made in the shop?
c) What are the disadvantages? (Think about the sources.)
d) Does this mean modern shops are better or worse? Explain your answer carefully.

3 a) Look at source C. Study the scene fully. Make detailed notes of what you can see.
b) For each note, write down how a modern street compares with this.

4 a) How many hours a week did the York guild members work? (Don't count meals. Assume seven and a half hours on Saturday.)
b) How many weeks' holidays did they have?
c) Ask your mother or father about their working week and their holidays. How do they compare with the figures on page 36?
d) Do they work more hours a year or fewer?

C People working at the same trade often had their shops in the same street. This picture shows stalls dealing in cloth and upholstery in 15th-century Italy.

8 LAW AND ORDER

There were no police in the Middle Ages. So tracking down criminals was a difficult job. Proving they had committed a crime was often even harder. The pictures above show some of the methods which were used to keep law and order.

Most cases wound up being tried in the manor courts. These courts dealt with local problems, such as letting your sheep trample someone's corn. The lord heard the case and made the final decision. William I had made sure these courts did their job properly.

However, as time passed, the barons grew more powerful. By the middle of the 12th century, barons often ignored the king's laws. They had become like kings on their own lands. And, of course, if you had a complaint against the baron, you stood almost no chance of a fair trial.

It was Henry II who improved the system and made sure it worked. Several times each year, he sent his own judges out from Westminster. They held trials in each county, and the county chose twelve men to form a jury. Originally, their job was to tell the judge all they knew about the people accused of crimes.

At first, it was not their job to decide if the person was guilty. They left that task to God. The method they used had changed little since the time of Edward the Confessor. The accused person had to go through an ordeal. God, they believed, would make sure that the guilty were found out.

There was a lot of luck involved in surviving an ordeal. In fact, ordeals could never find out the real truth about a crime. Even in the Middle Ages, people were having doubts about the method. Indeed, people found innocent by an ordeal were sometimes banished anyway – just to be on the safe side!

Three kinds of trial by ordeal. There was also an ordeal by boiling water.

1 a) Explain how each of these worked: ordeal by fire; ordeal by water; ordeal by battle.
b) For each one, suggest a reason why it might give the wrong verdict.

In 1215, the Pope said that priests must no longer help to organise ordeals. As a result, most ordeals were stopped. So the jury was given a new job. They had to decide if an accused person was innocent or guilty. Oddly, this was not popular at first. Some people thought they stood a worse chance of going free if their neighbours did not like them!

Like it or not, the accused person could not avoid a trial. After 1275, anyone who refused to go before a jury could be tortured.

A A courtroom of the Middle Ages.

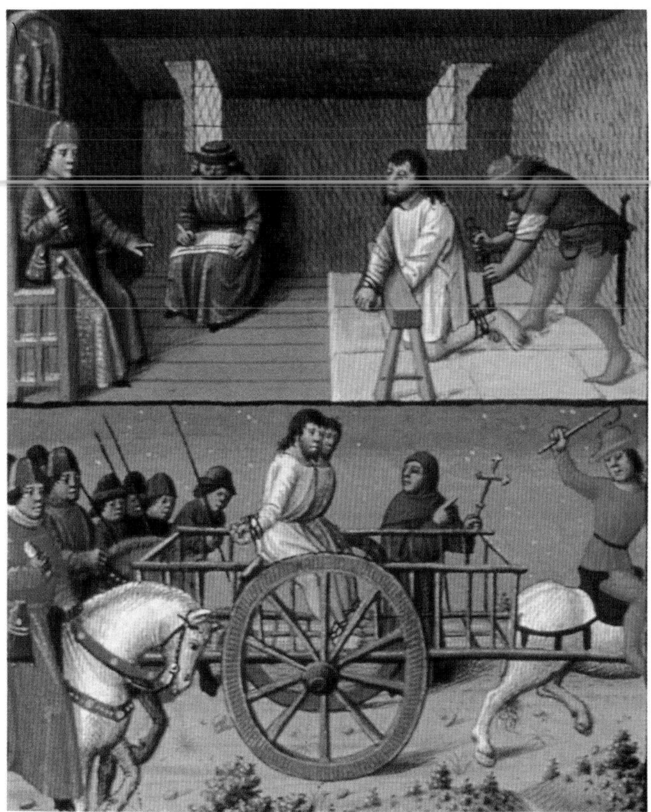

B Medieval pictures showing a trial (top) and the prisoner being taken to be punished (bottom).

C From a Coroner's Roll of 1266–7.

It happened about bedtime. Henry Colburn of Barford went out of his house in Barford to drink a tankard of beer and did not return that night. Early the next morning Agnes Colburn, his mother, looked for him and found the said Henry dead.

He was wounded about the heart and in the belly with seven knife-wounds, and in the head with four wounds apparently made with a pickaxe; also in the throat and the chin and the head as far as the brain.

Agnes at once raised the hue and cry and pursuit was made. And she finds pledges [promises]: Humphrey Quarrel and Thomas Quarrel of the same Barford.

2 a) What new form of ordeal did the Normans introduce?
b) Do you think this was an improvement? Give reasons.

3 a) Write down two later changes to trials.
b) Do you think these were improvements or not?
c) Did people at the time see them as improvements? Explain your answer.

4 a) Look at source A. Write down who you think you can see at the numbered places.
b) Look at source B. Is this earlier or later than source A? Explain how you decided.

PUNISHMENT

Medieval punishments were often violent and usually in public. People who hunted in royal forests had their ears cut off; thieves had their hands cut off; people selling bad goods were put in the stocks or the **pillory**. Wives who nagged their husbands were paraded round town in a bridle.

William I stopped the death penalty. Henry I brought it back again. Male murderers were hanged, although nobles could choose to have their heads cut off. A **gibbet** often stood just outside the town. Bodies hung there for weeks as a warning to other would-be criminals.

People waiting to be tried might spend the time in prison. But few people were sent to prison as a punishment. It cost too much money and there were too few prisons. Anyway, they were usually made of wood until the 13th century. It would have been too easy to escape from a wooden gaol, therefore prisoners weren't held in them for long.

The worst of crimes was **high treason**. So traitors were punished more brutally than anyone else. Women were often strangled and burnt, as female murderers were. But men were hanged and cut down while still alive. Before they died, their insides were taken out and burned before their eyes. The head was then cut off and the body cut into quarters. These might be sent off to four major towns to be displayed as a warning.

A A gaoler and his prisoners, from the *Holkham Bible*, made in about 1330. Prisoners had to provide their own food – or starve.

The sources on these pages give information about punishments in the Middle Ages. Read them before answering the questions on page 41.

B The stocks were often used as a public punishment. These monks had robbed a church. People were sometimes killed while in the stocks or died of exposure.

C A case of horse stealing, from *Le Court Baron* (13th century). It is a book of instructions for a lord's official on how to hold a court.

Steward: Bailiff!
Bailiff: Sir!
Steward: Why was this man taken?
Bailiff: Sir, for a mare which he took in the field of C, otherwise than he ought.
Steward: What is your name?
Defendant: Sir, my name is William.
Steward: William, now answer me how you came by this mare. You cannot deny that she was found with you, and that you said openly she was yours.
Defendant: Sir, I do not claim this mare and never saw her until now. These men have their hearts big against me and hate me much.
Steward: Do what is right and have God before your eyes. Confess the truth of this thing and the other things you have done.
Defendant: Sir, in God's name have pity on me and I will confess the truth. My great poverty and the devil's tempting made me steal this mare. Often they have made me do other things that I ought not to have done.
Steward: God pardon you! William, at least you have confessed in this court that you stole this mare and have done many other ill deeds. Will you say or confess anything else?
Defendant: Nay, sir.
Steward: Bailiff!
Bailiff: Sir!
Steward: Take him away, and let him have a priest. [This is a way of saying that the defendant will be hanged.]

D Medieval punishments were often chosen to fit the crime. This case was in 1364. The prosecutor said:

John Ryghtwys and John Penrose sold red wine to all who came there. [It was] unwholesome and deceived the common people. [The verdict was] that John Penrose shall drink a draught of the same red wine which he sold to the common people. The remainder of such wine shall then be poured on John's head. And he shall give up the trade of [wine merchant] in the City of London forever, unless he can obtain the King's favour.

E *The White Book of the City of London* (1419) listed these crimes which were punished by being put in the pillory.

Rotten meat . . . for a stinking rabbit sold . . . for pretending that he was a Sheriff's Serjeant, and placing the Bakers of Stratforde under arrest until they had paid a fine . . . for cutting a purse . . . for taking away a child, to go begging with him . . . for false dice, with which he played and deceived people . . . for begging under false pretences . . . for practising Magic . . . for placing a piece of iron in a loaf of bread . . .

F The execution of Hugh Despenser in 1326 was unusually violent. Before being hanged, drawn and quartered, he was crowned with nettles. A picture from a 14th-century chronicle.

G A public execution. Executions were public entertainments. People turned up in their best clothes to enjoy the sight.

H O G Tomkeieff, a historian, described crimes in Lincoln in 1202. There were . . .

about 430 cases of crime, including 114 cases of homicide, 89 of robbery (often with violence), 65 of wounding and 49 of rape. Only two criminals were hanged and between 20 and 30 outlawed. Most of the others paid fines, while some managed to reach sanctuary in a church. [Anyone claiming sanctuary was allowed to stay in the church. After 40 days, they were allowed to leave the country.]

Historians try to get as much information from their sources as they can. However, they must still ask:

- Who made it?
- When was it made?
- Why was it made?
- How reliable is it?

1 Take each source in turn. Write down what you can learn from it about punishments. For instance, for source B, you could write down: *The stocks were used to punish people in public.* Write at least one sentence about each source.

2 Look at the four questions above which historians ask about sources. Read the captions to sources A, B and H. What would a historian need to know about each source, apart from what is in the caption?

3 What do you learn from these sources about punishments? Write a detailed answer and quote from the sources – but do not copy out large sections of any one source. You should consider these points:
- where the punishments took place
- the kind of punishments
- how they compare with modern punishments.

9 FOREIGN TRADE

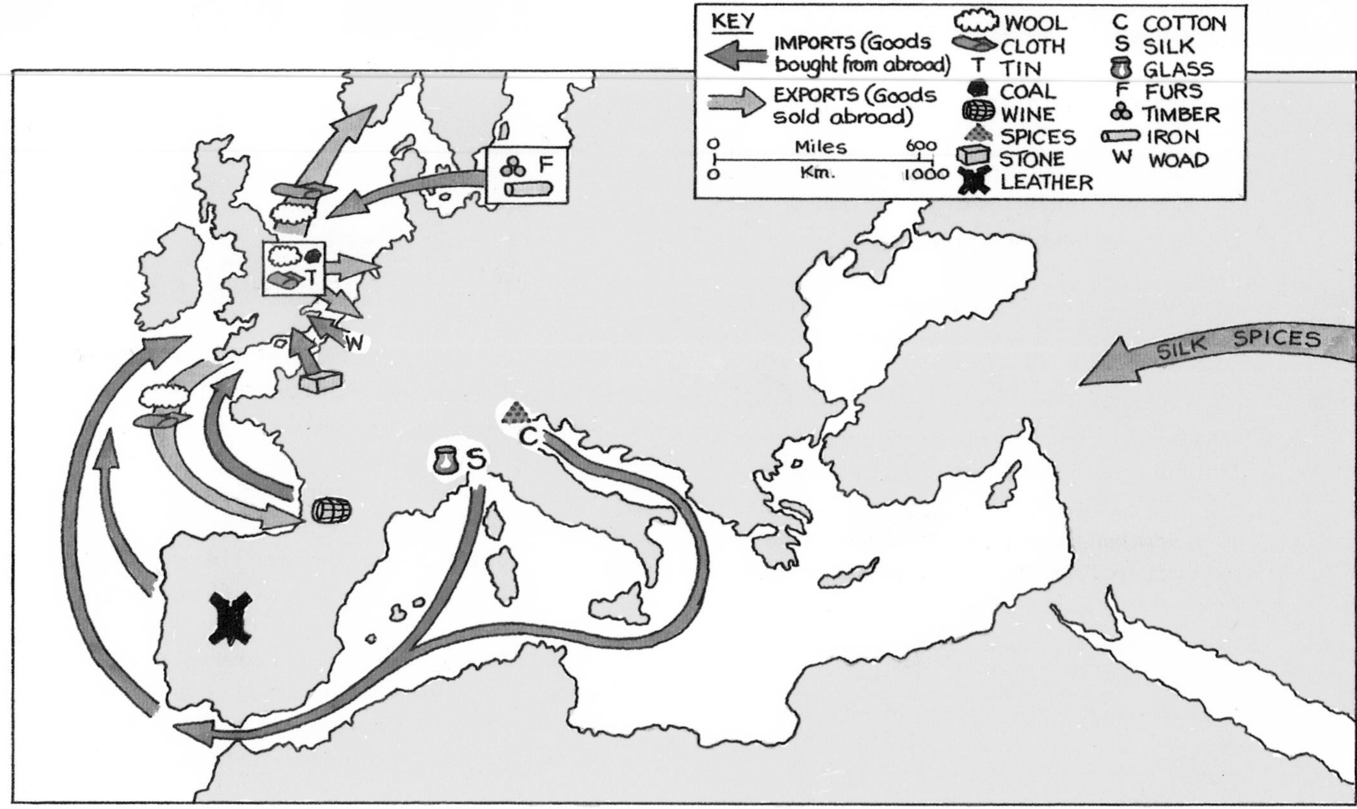

A This map shows some exports and imports in the Middle Ages.

Villagers tried to produce everything they needed. But there were a few things which they could not produce, such as salt. There were no refrigerators so they needed salt to preserve meat through the winter.

The lords and ladies enjoyed a glass of French wine; they liked to wear the finest foreign silk. Then, there were eastern spices which added flavour to all that salted meat. All these luxuries had to be bought. In return, the English sold goods abroad. What they mainly sold was wool and, later, cloth.

Sheep made the country rich. The biggest flocks were owned by the monasteries. In 1310, there were about three sheep for each human being.

English and Welsh wool was the finest in Europe. Foreign merchants toured the land, finding wool to buy. They were careful to check the quality. Welsh wool from Tintern Abbey was four times more valuable than wool from Gloucestershire. From the 12th century, wool was our biggest export.

English kings were quick to cotton on to the value of wool! They saw a way of making money for themselves. In 1275, Edward I fixed a customs duty of 33.5p on every sack of wool. In the 14th century, these taxes earned the king £10,000 a year.

The king's officials realised it was easier to collect this money if all exports went through one town. They called this the *staple* town. Different towns were chosen over the years. In 1363, it was fixed at Calais on the coast of France. The town belonged to England at that time.

During the 14th century, cloth began to replace wool as the main export. England was at war with France and this interrupted the wool trade. Anyway, selling cloth earned more money than selling raw wool.

Cloth-making provided work for villagers when they came home from the fields. Much of it was done by the women. They sheared the sheep and spun the wool. Everyone joined in the cleaning and weaving.

Wool and cloth also made the merchants rich. Richard Whittington became Lord Mayor of London three times. He used his money to help the old and sick and improved the water supplies. Other merchants were equally generous. The huge churches of East Anglia and the Cotswolds were built by rich wool merchants.

B The Cely family were rich wool merchants. In this letter of 1479, Richard Cely writes to his son George. It was normal for the elder family members to stay in Britain while the younger men worked abroad.

Let this letter be delivered to George Cely at Calais or Bruges.

I greet you well. I understand that you were very ill in Bruges. Your mother and both your brothers and Wyll Maryon and I were all sorry and concerned for you. I hope to God that you have now recovered and are fully healed.

John Cely has been in Cotswold and made up a [delivery] of thirty-seven sacks, for which I will need a good lot of canvas. You can buy for me four or five lengths of Burgen canvas, or Barras good quality. [Also] three dozen packs of Calais thread, as I will need them. If you can't, I will have to [buy] them in London. I'm advised to pack the wool between Christmas and Candlemas. I'm advised not to ship any wool before March.

I'll write nothing more for the present, but may Jesus keep you.

Written in London in haste, the sixth day of November.

Richard Cely

D There are many reminders that medieval Britain depended on wool. Pub signs such as these are common. Only in the 19th century did street names and house numbers become common. Signs were, therefore, very important for messengers.

C The great crane at Bruges. The name Bruges means 'landing-place'. It became the Scottish staple town in the 14th century.

1 a) Explain the meaning of these words: (i) import, (ii) export, (iii) customs duty and (iv) staple town.
b) Look at the map on page 42. What do you think people used these imports for: (a) salt (b) iron (c) stone (d) woad (blue dye).

2 a) Look at source C. How is the crane powered?
b) What goods do you think are being tested on the left?
c) What differences would you expect to find in a dockyard scene today?

3 a) Read source B. How does this letter differ from a modern one? (At least two answers.)
b) How is it similar to a modern one? (Again, two answers.)
c) You are George Cely. You try to buy the goods your father wants. You manage to buy the canvas, but not the thread. Write a letter to your father, explaining what has happened. (You can make up other details, about your health, for instance.) Make sure the letter is organised as the one in source B.

10 IN SICKNESS AND IN HEALTH

People in western Europe knew very little about curing disease – and that included the doctors! Many of their medical ideas had not changed in the previous 1000 years.

Medicine had not improved partly because the Church banned Christians from cutting up dead bodies. So it was difficult for doctors to learn more about how bodies work. Of course, some doctors ignored this ban. But western doctors were mostly more ignorant than those in eastern countries.

In any case, the Church did not encourage people to seek out new knowledge. Priests believed that the Bible taught people everything they needed to know. So experiments were quite unnecessary.

As a result, doctors had few ways of finding out what was wrong with people. The most basic was studying the patient and asking questions. If this did not work, the doctor could take the patient's pulse or take a urine sample. He checked it against a urine chart, like this one.

A

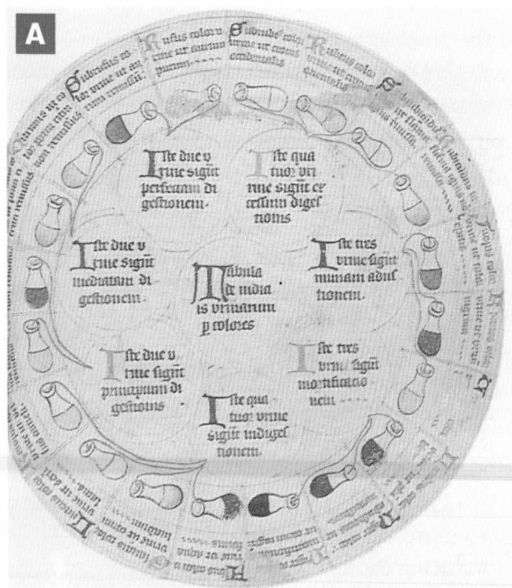

In fact, urine samples told doctors very little. But the doctor had one final method. He consulted the stars. A quick study of the patient's birth sign and the heavens above provided the answer!

However, few people ever saw a doctor. There was no National Health Service. Treatment cost money. The poor just couldn't afford it. Instead, the womenfolk usually looked after the sick.

They used herbs which they gathered themselves. Many of these were quite successful. The juice of poppy flowers was used to deaden pain. It contains morphine, a drug still used today.

B A woman surgeon delivers a baby after a difficult birth. She has done a Caesarian section, a method still used today. Few babies were this lucky: most were born on the cottage floor.

Religion even played a part in these home remedies. Priests taught people that illness was God's way of punishing them. So it was natural for them to pray to get better. People believed that epilepsy, for instance, was caused by the devil. One cure was to write the names of the three wise men on a piece of parchment. This was tied to a child's stomach to stop the fits.

Some people consulted the friars. If all else failed, a pilgrimage might be the answer. People travelled miles to pray at the shrines of saints, such as Thomas Becket. Others wore lucky charms or said magic spells.

However, all this was probably no worse than going to see a doctor. Having a visit from a doctor was very expensive. People usually visited a barber-surgeon, who was cheaper. You could spot his shop by the pole outside.

The barber-surgeons cut hair and performed small operations. They pulled out teeth and bled people to let 'bad' blood out of their body. But their instruments were not cleaned properly. Infection was a real risk.

However, people did not understand why they became ill. Filthy towns and dirty drinking water were part of their lives. So was illness. A few lucky people might find a bed in a hospital. But even hospitals were not clean by our standards.

C This 15th-century picture shows a hospital in Paris. It was founded in the 7th century.

D Part of a letter written in 1365 by one Italian to another.

I talked recently with a doctor, a very good friend of mine. I asked him why he did not practise medicine. He put on a sad and serious look, inspiring confidence in his judgement. He said, 'I am afraid of cheating the public. If people knew, as I do, how little, if at all, the doctor helps the patient, the company of [doctors] would be much smaller. Let them act [as they wish]; let them promise life, and kill, and make money. But I have no intention of cheating and killing; I don't want to get richer by doing any man harm.'

Medieval people did not know about germs – so they could not know that germs caused illness. If they could not see the reason for the illness, they often assumed it was a punishment from God.

E Medieval cures. (These have been put into modern English.)

For tonsilitis:
Take a fat cat and skin it. Mix together hedgehog grease, bear fat, herbs, honeysuckle and wax. Stuff the cat with the mixture, then roast it. Take the grease and rub it in.

Recipe for an ointment:
Collect some crickets and cut off the heads and wings. Put them in a pot of oil, along with some dung-beetles. Heat the mixture, then crush it and rub it on any painful parts.

When praying at a healing well:
Take a cockerel for a boy or a hen for a girl. Throw 4d [about 1.5p] into the well and say the Lord's prayer. The disease will pass out of the child into the bird.

To avoid having a baby:
Wear a red thread round your neck.

1 a) Doctors had four ways of finding out what was wrong with people. What were they?
b) Which one is not used today?
c) Why do you think they have stopped doing this?

2 a) Look at source C. What clues are there that the Church helped to run this hospital?
b) What evidence is there that people were not always cured?
c) What shows that the nuns did not understand how diseases were spread?
d) Why didn't they understand this?

3 Do you think *all* people in the Middle Ages:
a) Believed prayers would make them better.
b) Trusted doctors to make them better.
c) Believed cutting up dead bodies was wrong.
d) Thought doctors were ignorant.
Explain each answer carefully.

4 Work in pairs. One of you is a medieval villager; the other is a modern doctor. The doctor must explain what is wrong about medieval medicine and that some diseases are caused by germs. The villager must reply, using the knowledge people then had. Plan your ideas first. You might then tape your conversation.

THE GREAT DEATH

Look back at the Paris hospital on page 45. In 1348, the nuns were coping with a great problem. People were dying of a horrible disease. There was nothing new about this. What was different this time was the huge number of people who caught the disease. They called it 'the Great Death'.

That summer, two French ships arrived at the little Dorset port of Melcombe. One of the sailors had the disease. Soon, people in England caught it. The disease spread rapidly across southern England.

A A writer called Boccaccio saw the effects in Italy. He described the symptoms:

At the beginning, both men and women were affected by a sort of swelling in the groin or under the armpits, which sometimes reached the size of a common apple or egg.

Some of these swellings were larger than this and some were smaller. They were commonly called boils. From these two starting-points, the boils began in a little while to spread all over the body.

Later the appearance of the disease changed to black or red patches on the arms and thighs. These blotches quickly led to death.

Most people who caught the disease died quickly – in just two to five days. No wonder people were terrified. 'Our Father,' they prayed, 'let the deadly disease fall on others.' And it did. By autumn, it was in London. By 1349, Wales and Scotland were affected. In Ireland, the population of Dublin was almost destroyed.

B Many people believed the disease was caused by arrows sent by God, as in this 15th-century Italian painting.

C Victims being buried. Later, there was no time for coffins. Bodies were just thrown into large pits.

No one could understand why it spread so quickly. It seemed to appear in places for no reason at all, places which were far away from any town or village. Doctors were helpless.

Today, most historians believe that the disease was the plague – and there were two kinds of it. One was spread by fleas which lived on the bodies of black rats. Their bites caused the swellings, known as buboes. These lumps give the disease its modern name: bubonic plague. No one would have noticed a flea-bite. People were used to being bitten by fleas.

The other was spread from person to person, by coughing and sneezing. This kind of plague was nearly always fatal.

The rats hid in bales of corn and straw which were carted across country. The fastest transport was the horse-drawn wagon. The rats simply hitched a ride. Others walked from farmhouse to farmhouse, infecting other rats on the way.

What Caused the Great Death?

Wild rumours spread about what caused the disease. Some people thought you could get it by over-eating. Sources D to I are explanations from primary sources.

D Guy de Chauliac, a French doctor:
The cause was the close position of the three planets, Saturn, Jupiter and Mars. This had taken place on the 24th March 1345. Such coming together of planets is always a sign of wonderful, terrible or violent things to come.

E de Smet:
It was thought that the whole area was infected through the foul blast of wind that came from the south.

F Jean de Venette:
The plague spread because of contagion : if a healthy man visited a plague victim, he usually died himself. It spread invisibly from house to house and finally from person to person.

G A monk living in Flanders:
In the East, near India there were horrors and storms for three days. On the first day, frogs, snakes, lizards and scorpions fell from the sky. On the second day there was thunder and lightning. On the third day, fire and stinking smoke came down from heaven. This killed all the remaining men and animals and destroyed all the towns.

H Geoffrey le Baker:
Hardly anyone would dare touch a person with the disease. The remains of the dead were shunned by the healthy, for they were tainted with the plague.

I Matthew of Neuenberg:
[A person] rose and read a letter out loud. In [it], the angel said that Christ was displeased by the wickedness of the world, and named many sins: not observing Sunday, not fasting on Friday, blasphemy , usury [money-lending], adultery.

J In 1894, doctors discovered that bubonic plague is caused by germs carried by fleas – the fleas which live on black rats. When the rat died, the flea looked for a new home.

K This photograph shows people dying from plague in China in 1911. From time to time, the disease still broke out in the 20th century.

Nowadays, we call this event 'the Black Death'. Medieval people did not use this term – or the word 'plague'. They spoke of the Great Mortality – in other words, the Great Death. (The Scots called it the Foul Death.) The Black Death is a nickname given to it centuries later.

1 Look at each of the explanations for the plague (D –I). Remember that there were two kinds of plague in 1348–9. Give each explanation a mark out of ten to show how right you think it is. For instance, if you think source D is the best reason, give it ten marks.

2 a) Why do modern writers not believe the reasons given by sources B and D?
b) Why do you think people at the time *did* believe these reasons?
c) Would it have helped them to know that the disease was spread by fleas? Explain your answer.

3 Source J is what most people believe today. Does that mean it must be correct? Explain your answer carefully.

4 As a class, compare your answers to question 1. How similar are your marks?

AFTER THE GREAT DEATH

Historians do not agree on how serious the plague was. Priests and doctors certainly suffered badly. In fact, some doctors refused to visit patients. In some areas, nearly one priest in two was killed by the disease.

Towns suffered most. In 1347, about 70,000 people lived in London. During 1348 and 1349, probably nearly half of them died. Some villages were wiped out. Thirty years later, a tax collector could find no one living in the Yorkshire village of Bolton.

This photograph shows where the village of Tusmore, in Oxfordshire, used to be. There were 23 households here before the plague came. In 1357, the King let the local lord use it as a park. There was no one left to farm it.

Lords had relied on most of their farmwork being done by peasants in return for land. Now, there were fewer peasants. The lords had to pay extra workers to sow the seed and get the harvest in.

B Landlords soon found that these labourers wanted extra pay. John Gower wrote this in *The Mirror of Man* in about 1375.

The world goes fast from bad to worse. Labour is now so high a price that a landlord must pay 25–30p for what cost 10p in the past. Labourers of old did not eat wheat bread; they had beans or coarser corn bread, and their drink was water alone. Cheese and milk were a feast to them. Now they work little, dress and feed like their betters. Ruin stares us in the face.

C The lord of the manor of Cuxham in Oxfordshire certainly had this problem. This graph is based on figures in the manor records. It shows the number of days' work done by the peasants for the lord.

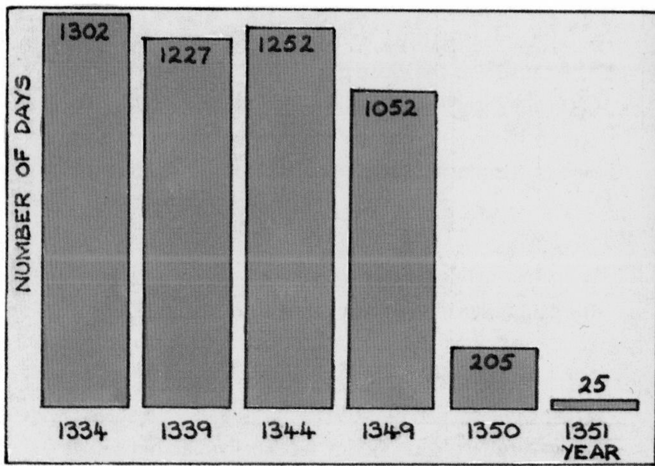

That summer of 1348, farm animals wandered along empty streets and ate the corn and beans. Dead animals lay rotting in the fields. People were too terrified of death to worry much about looking after their animals.

Prices dropped suddenly. Who wanted to worry about breeding animals when you might be dead tomorrow?

However, by 1349, prices were rising again. After all, the survivors had to eat. But less food had been produced in 1348. People had been too worried about the plague. Now, they needed food. And lords needed workers. So workers demanded higher pay – four times as much, in some cases.

D Twice, the King tried to hold down wages. This is a summary of part of the Statute of Labourers (1351).

All servants shall earn the same as they did in 1347. They shall not be paid by the day.
Wages for hay-making shall not be more than 1p a day.
Labourers must be hired openly in towns.
No one may leave the town where they normally live in winter during the summer.
People must swear an oath to obey this law. Anyone refusing must be put in the stocks or sent to gaol.
Wages of carpenters, masons and tilers must be the same as in 1347. The same with plasterers who should not be given free food or drink.
Any extra wages must be paid back.

By and large, these laws did not work. Some landowners avoided paying higher wages. They kept sheep instead of growing crops. They needed fewer workers to look after sheep. Others gave the peasants their freedom. They paid them wages and charged rent for the land they gave them.

The Church suffered badly. More of the priests had died than any other group in the land. If God was punishing the wicked, people thought, priests must have been pretty awful people!

After the Black Death, it was not easy to find someone willing to become a priest. Many of the new priests had little or no education. They were not the kind of people to make villagers trust the Church.

E Throughout Europe, there was a sense of doom. This was shown in the art of the time. Sculptures on tombs showed corpses crawling with worms. So did paintings like this one.

The Bishop of Winchester had a particular problem. He had just knocked down the west front of the cathedral when the disease struck. The plague left the Church short of money. His solution was a temporary new front. It is still there.

F

How many people died? The truth is that no one knows. There was no census in the Middle Ages. So we do not know exactly how many people there were before the Black Death.

Writers at the time gave very vague figures. They probably exaggerated. One writer said that just one in ten survived. But he may have been writing about those who *caught* the plague.

Another writer thinks that only one person in 20 died in the countryside. Others think that, on average, one person in three died. If that is true, a soldier in the First World War stood a better chance of surviving than a peasant in 1348.

Historians never rely on just one source. They compare sources to find out what happened in the past. One source may not tell the whole truth.

1 Why would it be dangerous only to rely on: (a) source A; (b) source C; (c) the cartoon?

2 On the other hand, what can you learn from: (a) source A; (b) source C; (c) the cartoon?

3 Is source B biased? Explain your answer.

4 a) Look at source E. What does this tell you about people's *feelings* about the plague?
b) How would it affect people going to church?
c) Why do you think artists made pictures like these?

5 a) Note briefly the effects of the Black Death. Put one on each line.
b) Now, decide which was most important and put it at the top of the list.
c) Write about the effects of the Black Death. Include one paragraph about each of the points you noted in (a).

11 THE PEASANTS' REVOLT

1000 1100 1200 1300 1400 1500

A This primary source shows a French peasants' revolt in 1358 – 13 years before the peasants revolted in England.

In June 1381, an army of peasants marched from Kent into London. Another group arrived from Essex. They captured the Tower of London. They murdered the Archbishop of Canterbury and the King's Treasurer.

King Richard II was just 14 years old. He met the rebels twice to listen to their complaints. What were they complaining about? These two pages look at the causes of their revolt.

1 They wanted freedom on the manor

After the Black Death, many lords gave the peasants their freedom. The lords paid the peasants for their work; the peasants paid rent for their land. In some counties, the lords fought hard to stop this. In others, such as Kent, many peasants already had their freedom. They did not want the lords taking it away again.

2 Criticism of the Church

The Church was one of the biggest landowners of all. The bishops were determined that the peasants should not be given their freedom. John Wycliffe had criticised the Church for being so rich. Wycliffe himself did not encourage the peasants. But the peasants were well aware of the views of other critics. One of these was John Ball.

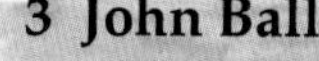

3 John Ball

John Ball was a priest in Kent. He was not allowed to preach in churches. So he preached in the open air instead. Every Sunday, he told the peasants things like, 'Matters cannot go well in England until everyone is treated equally.' It was, of course, just what the peasants wanted to hear.

4 Long wars against France
England had been fighting France, off and on, since 1340. Long wars always bring misery. There had already been a revolt by French peasants.

5 The poll tax
Long wars meant the King needed more money. In 1380, Richard II introduced another tax. It was called the poll (head) tax because every adult had to pay 5p, whether they were rich or poor. It was the third poll tax in just four years. Even so, it did not bring in the money that the King expected.

6 The tax-collectors arrive
In May 1381, an official called Bampton turned up in Essex. He wanted to know why the villagers of Fobbing had not paid their poll tax. The villagers threw him out.

Next month, soldiers arrived. But, by then, the villagers were organised. They had rounded up supporters from other villages. This time, the soldiers were thrown out. Within days, villagers in Kent also revolted. The march towards London began.

Historians try to work out why events happened. In other words, they try to find out the causes. Some causes are long-term – such as problems which have lasted for years. But sometimes events are caused by things which happened immediately beforehand. These are called short-term causes. Most events are caused by a mixture of the two.

1 a) Please work in groups. Take a large sheet of paper and divide it into two. On the left, write **Long-term causes**. On the right, write **Short-term causes**. In each column, write down as many causes as you can find for the Peasants' Revolt.
b) Now, turn back to page 49. Find another cause of the revolt. Decide which column to put it in.
c) At the end of the lesson, some groups can present their ideas to the class. First, answer question 2.

2 a) Look at source A. An English lord hears about this revolt. How will it affect his feelings about his own peasants?
b) An English peasant hears about this revolt. How will it affect his feelings about his lord?
c) Would their feelings have been different if they *saw* this scene? Give reasons.

B John Ball with the peasants. This is a French picture, made nearly 100 years later. What weapons would you expect peasants to have?

A The meeting at Smithfield. This picture was painted nearly 100 years after the event. It comes from Froissart's *Chronicles*. This is the same source as B (on page 51). Two events are shown here. On the right, the King talks to the peasants. The scene on the left is described in sources D and E.

THE REVOLT ENDS

By now, the rebels had leaders. The Kent rebels were led by Wat Tyler. Along the way, they freed John Ball who had been in Maidstone gaol. They destroyed records of peasants' duties; they burned houses where the records were kept.

When the peasants arrived outside London, the gates of the city were thrown open. Many Londoners supported them. Wat Tyler said there should be no looting. But, soon, many rebels were drunk. Buildings were burned down. Foreigners were murdered.

On 14 June, the King met the rebels at Mile End. They told him that they wanted to be free from their lords. All the old duties should be stopped. Instead, they wanted to rent land at 4d (1.5p) an acre.

The King agreed to these demands and asked the peasants to go home. Some did. Meanwhile, another group headed for the Tower of London. The peasants had also asked the King to punish all traitors. But he had refused.

That same day, there was a dreadful slaughter. The Archbishop of Canterbury and the King's Treasurer were dragged from the Tower of London. The rebels cut off their heads on Tower Hill.

The young King spent the night in hiding. Next day, he rode out once more to meet the rebels, led by Wat Tyler. They met at Smithfield, a grassy area outside the city. (The word means 'smooth field'.)

The rebels did not write about these events. Our sources were written by people who were all on the King's side. They tell much the same story, but they do not agree on details. Few of them actually saw the events. So it is difficult to decide which version is most accurate. For instance, read these two accounts of the meeting at Mile End.

B *The City Letter Book* described what happened.

All the men from Kent and Essex met at the place called 'Mileende', together with some of the wicked persons from the city. The King came to them from the Tower, accompanied by many knights and esquires. The lady his mother followed him in a chariot.

At the request of the angry crowd, our Lord the King granted that they might take those who were traitors against him.

C Sir John Froissart described the same meeting in his *Chronicles*.

The King advanced into the midst of the crowd, saying in a most pleasing manner, 'My good people, I am your king and your lord. What is it you want?'

[They replied,] 'We wish you to make us free for ever. We wish to be no longer called slaves.' The King replied, 'I grant your wish; now therefore return to your homes. Let two or three from each village be left behind, to whom I will order letters to be given with my seal, granting every demand you have made.'

D During the meeting at Smithfield, Wat Tyler was killed. This is how the *City Letter Book* described the event:

In front of the King, with the lords and knights on one hand and the angry mob on the other, Sir William Walworthe (the Mayor) bravely rushed upon Walter Tylere while he was arguing with the King and nobles. He first wounded him in the neck, then threw him from his horse, fatally wounding him in the chest.

E Sir John Froissart said the event began with an argument between Wat Tyler and a royal squire. This, said Froissart, is what happened next:

The Mayor of London arrived with twelve knights, all well-armed, and broke through the crowd. He said to Tyler, 'Ha! Would you dare to speak like that in front of the King?' The King began to get angry and told the Mayor, 'Set hands on him.' Tyler said to the Mayor, 'What have I said to annoy you?' 'You lying, stinking, crook,' said the Mayor, would you speak like that in front of the King? By my life, you'll pay dearly for it.'

And the Mayor drew out his sword and struck Tyler such a blow on the head that he fell down at the feet of his horse. The knights clustered round him so he could not be seen by the rebels. Then a squire called John Standish drew out his sword and put it into Tyler's belly and so he died.

F Thomas Walsingham described what happened to John Ball in his *English History*.

John Ball was brought to St Albans, tried and hanged [July 15] . . .

On St Margaret's Day [July 20], the King was amazed to hear that the bodies of those hanged at St Albans had been daringly taken from the gallows. So he sent a writ, requesting them to be replaced in chains to hang as long as they lasted.

None would do the work for [the peasants]. With their own hands they had to hang up their fellow citizens whose rotting bodies were full of maggots and stank. It was fitting for [these] men to have the disgusting task whereby they earned the apt name of 'hangmen', to their lasting shame.

1 What part did these people play in the revolt: Wat Tyler; John Ball; William Walworth?

2 a) Read sources B and C. Write down the main differences between them.
b) Do you think the writers are for or against the peasants? Explain how you decided.

3 a) Read sources D and E. Write down the main differences between them.
b) Do you think the writers are for or against the peasants? Explain how you decided. (A different reason for each source.)

4 a) Was Thomas Walsingham for or against the peasants? Give reasons.
b) Look at your answers to 2b, 3b and 4a. Why does this make finding out what happened difficult?

5 Read the caption to source A. Does this source help us to discover the truth? Explain your answer carefully.

The revolt was mostly over by the end of the summer. These pictures show what happened afterwards.

12 EDUCATION

A Girls were often taught in nunneries. These were the lessons recommended in one book in 1371.

It is impossible to know how many medieval people could read – or how much they could read. Most people could probably read a few lines of Latin at least. If they did, few learned to do this at school. They must have picked it up from their parents or perhaps the local priest.

If a villein's child wanted to enter the Church, the lord had to give his permission. Until the 14th century, most schools for young children were run by the Church. Song schools trained choirboys for the church choir. These pupils learned to read Latin. The teachers were often asked to take on girls, too.

Older pupils went on to a grammar school. It was called this because Latin grammar was the main subject. All books were hand-written, so they were expensive. The teacher might have a book, but pupils learned lessons by heart. Dictionaries did not yet exist.

A noble's young children did not go to school. Mothers taught the daughters. A priest might teach the baron's son. When they were older, they were sent away to another noble's house. Girls and boys were taught to read and write. The boys also learned to hunt, ride and use weapons. They were taught to serve at table. (Noblemen always served the ladies then.)

The girls, on the other hand, spent their time learning to play music and to sew and dance. They were taught how to deal with servants and run a household. Like peasant girls, they were often married long before they were 14.

In the early Middle Ages, school was mainly for those who wanted to become priests or lawyers. But, after the Black Death, there was a shortage of priests. So William of Wykeham started a new school at Winchester to train priests. Young boys came from all over the country to live at the school.

They worked long days. In summer, they were up at 4 am. A service was followed by work until 9 am. The younger boys then had breakfast. Older boys waited until noon for their first meal! Afternoon lessons ended with supper at 6pm.

Long hours of learning by heart grew boring. The only way teachers could keep control was by regular beatings. You were beaten if you misbehaved. You were beaten for a single mistake in translation.

But schools, like so much else, changed during the Middle Ages. At first, some teachers spoke only in Latin, although others used French. But, after the Black Death, some teachers began teaching in English. It spelled the end of Latin as a living language – and the start of English as a language for everyone.

B Rules at King's College, Cambridge in the 15th century tried to stop scholars looking like this. Students could go to university at 14. Many had left by the age of 16.

C King Louis IX of France having lessons. His mother, Blanche, is seated on the left.

D From the inquest on John de Neushom, a teacher, in 1301.

John de Neushom went after dinner to find rods for beating his pupils. He climbed up a willow to cut rods next to the mill pond and fell in by accident and was drowned. The jurors say on oath that nobody was to blame for his death.

E John of Trevisa wrote this in 1385. It explains how English was started in grammar schools. This is the original spelling so you can see what the English of the time looked like.

Iohn Cornwaile, a maister of grammer, chaunged the lore in gramer scole and construccioun of Frensche in to Englische. Richard Pencriche lerned the menere techynge of hym and othere men of Pencrich; so that now, the year of oure Lorde a thowsand thre hundred and foure score and fyve, in alle the gramere scoles of Engelonde, children leue Frensche and construe and lerne in Englische.

[The] auauntage is that they lerne her gramer in lasse tyme than children were i-woned to doo; disauauntage is that now children of gramer scole conneth na more Frensche than can hir lift heele.

F Sir John Froissart described his schooldays in his *Chronicles* (14th century).

When I was grown a little wise, then I must needs be more fully subject to my masters; for they taught me the Latin tongue. If I varied in repeating my lessons, I was beaten.

I could not rest, for I fought with other children, beat and was beaten. I often went home with torn clothes; there again I was [told off] often or beaten.

1 As a class, work out what source E says. Remember that the letter 'v' was often written as 'u'. What other differences can you all spot?

2 How do these features of your school differ from a medieval one: (a) the lessons taught; (b) the hours of the day; (c) discipline?

3 a) What can you learn from sources D and F about medieval schools?
b) What can you *not* learn from these sources?
c) What *other* sources would you need to find out about these things?

4 a) Look at source A. What view of women do you think this writer had?
b) Do you think Blanche (in source C) would have shared these views? Explain how you decided.

13 THE BIRTH OF ENGLISH

The English language is a bit like a stew. It took 1000 years and three invasions to make it. It began with Anglo-Saxon. Christian missionaries then brought a flavouring of Latin; the Vikings added a dash of Danish spice. Finally, the Normans were left to cook it the French way and – hey presto, we have English!

William the Conqueror spoke Norman French. (He had a go at learning English, but was too busy.) For over 250 years afterwards, the language of government was French. It was the language of monarchs, too. (But you called them sovereigns, if you were French.) Documents were written in French or Latin. At first, church services were still held in Latin.

But the English went on speaking English. You can see this most clearly in our words for food.

A Most farm animals were still known by the old Saxon names (in red). The food they produce is known by Norman names (in blue).

However, the situation was even more complicated than that. Although the English all spoke English, there were huge differences between one area and another. What was spoken in one region sounded like a foreign language to people from elsewhere.

During the 14th century, some southern sailors were shipwrecked in the north. They asked for food, speaking in English. But the local people could not understand them and thought they were French. So they killed them.

What brought the two languages together was marriage. The Norman rulers married English women. Henry I was the first Norman king to speak some English. He had an English wife.

The king who did most to kill off French was King John. (Not that he planned it that way!) When he lost land in France, English nobles no longer had to worry about affairs across the Channel.

During the 14th century, French began to lose the battle. In 1362, for the first time, Parliament was opened in English. Even so, the King, Edward III, could only swear in English!

But what these people spoke was not *our* English. Experts call it Middle English. (Source E on page 55 is written in Middle English.) Two men played a major part in making this our English.

B What's in a name? Some older English names are on the left. The ones on the right were introduced after 1066.

The first was a poet called Geoffrey Chaucer. In the 1380s, he wrote a long poem about people going to Canterbury on a pilgrimage. We call it 'The Canterbury Tales'. The language he used was Middle English.

Long wars against France began in 1337. People began to think of French as the language of the enemy. When the wars ended in 1453, everyone was speaking English. By then, many people were writing in English, too.

The second man in the story is William Caxton. Round about 1476, he started the first printing press in England. He had a problem. What sort of English should he use in his books? Whatever kind he chose, some people would not understand it.

He sat in his study and did some translation. Afterwards, when he read it through, he wondered whether people would understand it. And he remembered a story about some merchants who were at sea. They landed to get some food.

C He later printed the story of what happened:

One of theym named Sheffelde came in-to an hows and axed for mete; and specyally he axyd after eggys. And the goode wyf answerde, that she coude speke no frenshe. And the marchaunt was angry, for he also coude speke no frenshe, but wolde have hadde egges, and she understode hym not. And thenne at laste a nother sayd that he wolde have eyren. Then the good wyf sayd that she understod hym wel.

Loo, what sholde a man in thyse dayes now wryte, egges or eyren? Certaynly it is harde to playse every man.

This was the version of English which Caxton decided to use. It was the English spoken in London, where he lived. What he chose is the basis of the English we speak and write today. Of course, people still speak with different accents. And each region has its own special words.

In the following century, British travellers took the English language across the Atlantic Ocean. Today, 500 years later, English is spoken by a billion people – that's about one-sixth of the world.

English is, too, probably the richest language in the world. There are more than half-a-million English words, not counting technical ones. That's nearly three times as many words as in German. And five times as many as in French. For that, we have to thank all those invaders who added to the English stew.

Probably every one of those billion people has at least some trouble getting the spelling right. If that includes you, you can blame printers like Caxton. They were printing books in English before writers and teachers had agreed how to spell the words. Anyway, as you can see in source C, his own spelling was erratic at times!

D Chaucer reading his poetry in Windsor.

1 Write about the part each of the following played in developing English:
a) Wars against France from 1337–1453
b) King John
c) Geoffrey Chaucer
d) William Caxton.

2 Look at source A. Match up the meats with the correct animal. (Be careful. There is a catch!)

3 a) Read source C. Write out the first three sentences in modern English.
b) Pass your version to a friend. Is it spelled correctly?
c) What do you notice about Caxton's spelling?

4 Look at the cartoon on page 56. Think very carefully. Can we be sure that *Ancren Riwle* was the first book in English? Explain your answer.

14 SCOTLAND

A Scotland in the Middle Ages.

Scotland was an independent country for most of the Middle Ages. The people lived in tribes, which they called *clans*. They were fierce fighters and were determined not to be conquered.

However, Norman customs and ways had been introduced into the Lowlands just across the border. Norman barons went to live there and built castles. Norman monks built monasteries.

Despite this, for most people, life did not change. As in England, this was true of farming. Lowland farmers ploughed strips (called *rigs*), just as English farmers did. But Highland farmers stuck to keeping animals.

Some changes came more slowly to Scotland. The feudal system came to Scotland 60 years after England. Some English towns were collecting their own taxes over a century before the first Scottish **burghs**. In the 14th century, all the taxes of Edinburgh came to just £35.

In 1286, the Scottish King died. There was no obvious person to take over, so the Scots asked King Edward I to decide. He agreed, as long as the Scots accepted him as their overlord. The Scottish Parliament unwillingly agreed.

The man Edward chose was John Baliol, an important landowner. However, once he was King, Baliol rebelled. Edward's soldiers marched into Scotland and defeated the Scots. Just to prove it, he brought back the Stone of Scone. This was an ancient stone on which Scottish kings were crowned. Edward put it in Westminster Abbey. It is still there under the coronation chair today.

The next year, 1297, a Scottish knight called William Wallace fought back. But in 1298, the Scots were beaten at Falkirk. Some years later, a Scottish traitor betrayed Wallace to the English. Wallace was hung, drawn and quartered. His limbs were put on display in four different places to warn the Scots.

But the Scots fought on. Their new leader was Robert Bruce. After Edward I's death in 1307, Robert won back many Scottish castles from the English. In the end, Edward II had to act. In 1314, an English army of 20,000 men moved north. It was, said eye-witnesses, the greatest English army they had ever seen.

B The Battle of Bannockburn. This 14th-century picture shows Robert Bruce killing Sir Henry Bohun with a battleaxe.

The two sides met on marshy land at Bannockburn. The English knights in their heavy armour simply got bogged down. The battle became a rout. Edward II fled from the battlefield.

The victory meant Scotland was free. In 1320, the Scottish nobles met at Arbroath. There, they wrote a letter to the Pope. It said that Edward had started the fighting. Now, Scotland was free again. Freedom, they said, was the greatest thing a country could have – and they kept it for the rest of the Middle Ages.

C From the Declaration of Arbroath (1320).

As long as one hundred men remain alive, we shall never submit to the rule of the English. It is not for glory, or riches, or honours that we fight, but for freedom alone, which no good man gives up but with his life.

Even today, the Scots still call the English *sassenachs*. It is an old Gaelic word, meaning 'Saxons'.

1 Draw a timeline for the years 1280 to 1330. Use 2 cms for each decade. On your timeline, write down what happened in these years: 1320; 1297; 1329; 1286; 1314.

2 a) Did Scotland change in the same ways as England changed? Give reasons.
b) How were the Lowlands different to the Highlands?

3 a) In pairs, write a short poem about Robert Bruce's victory at Bannockburn. One of you should write from the Scottish point of view; one of you should be English.
b) Collect up all the poems from your class. The teacher should now hand out the poems at random.
c) Look at the one you receive. Do you think this was written by a Scot or an English person? Write down how you decided.
d) What does this activity teach you about bias?

D On the left: This huge statue of Robert Bruce still stands at Bannockburn. He died in 1329 of leprosy.

Bruce and Ireland

With the English defeated, Robert Bruce now turned his attention to Ireland. His idea was to make his brother Edward King of Ireland. To do that, he had to defeat the Norman barons who held much of the land.

Norman barons had first turned up in Ireland during Henry II's reign. The country was split up into small kingdoms. The kings were almost always at war with each other. One of them, King Dermot, asked for help from England. A baron called Strongbow set out to assist.

In 1171, Dermot died. By then, Strongbow controlled Dublin. He had also married Dermot's daughter and now took over his kingdom. But Henry II had no intention of letting one of his own barons rule an independent kingdom.

So, later that year, he went personally to Ireland. Strongbow swore he would be loyal to Henry. In return, he kept much of his land. Some Irish kings also promised the English king their loyalty. In effect, Henry became Ireland's overlord.

The Normans used the same tactics to keep the Irish under control that they used in England. Wooden motte and bailey castles appeared throughout the land. Later, stone castles were built to replace them.

This was the Ireland which Edward and Robert Bruce tried to conquer. Some Irish chiefs had promised to support them. During bitter fighting, town after town was burned to the ground. It went on until Edward Bruce was defeated and killed in 1318.

The whole adventure brought great suffering to the Irish. It had also taught the English a lesson: Ireland was not yet safe. It was a problem which later English rulers would also have to face.

15 WALES

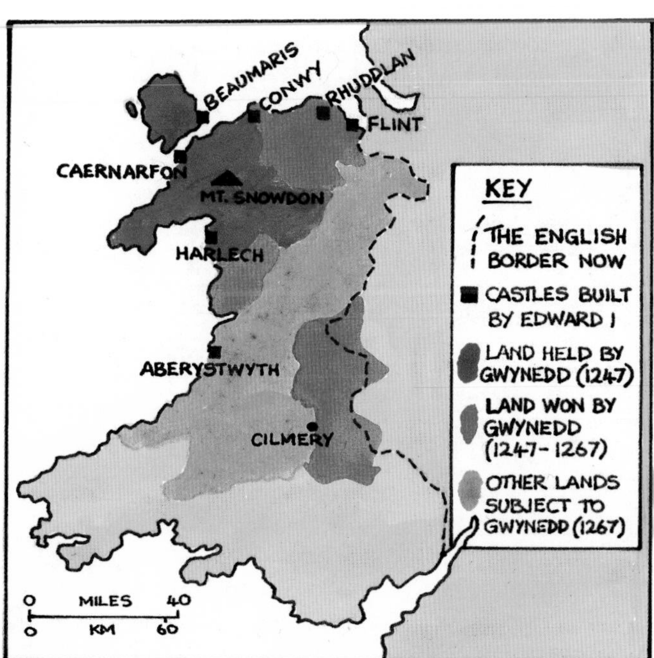

A Wales, showing the rise of Gwynedd and the castles of Edward I.

William I did not try to conquer Wales. But he did allow the local Norman barons to grab any land in Wales they wished. They captured the best Welsh farmland in the lowland areas. Soon, Norman castles appeared on their new lands.

But the Welsh were not easy to bring under control. They still lived in tribes and often fought each other. Their ancestors were the ancient Britons. These people had fled west when the Vikings arrived. The word 'Welsh' actually means 'foreigner'.

And foreigners they remained. In the area of Gwynedd, in the north, the princes banded together. They won back land from the English. By 1267, a Welsh prince called Llywelyn was recognised as 'Prince of Wales'. At that time, half the land was still controlled by local princes.

But in 1272, Edward I became king. He had other plans. Llywelyn refused to accept Edward as his overlord. So Edward led an English army into Wales and surrounded Llywelyn near Snowdon. Unable to get food, Llywelyn had to give in.

However, four years later, Llywelyn was back in action. It did not last long. Llywelyn was killed in the fighting and his head was stuck up at the Tower of London. The Welsh called their dead prince, 'Llywelyn our Last Leader'. Within a year, the revolt collapsed.

King Edward I did not intend to let the Welsh revolt again. So he built great castles in the land. They were the greatest fortresses since Roman times. Workmen were brought from all over England to build them. The total cost was huge – about £100,000.

There were ten of these castles – and another twelve smaller forts. Five of them had towns built around them. Edward encouraged English people to go and live there.

Conwy and Caernarfon Castles were planned for the King's use. It was at Caernarfon that Eleanor, Edward's wife, gave birth to their son, later Edward II. There, when he was 16, he was given the title of Prince of Wales. Ever since, the English ruler's eldest son has been given the title.

B Edward II being made Prince of Wales by his father at Caernarfon.

After years of peace, there was a final attempt at rebellion. In 1400, a squire called Owain Glyndŵr began 15 years of fighting against the English. The Welsh people suffered greatly. But, in the end, the English won. Glyndŵr himself became an outlaw and went into hiding. He was the last Welshman to lead his people against the English.

But that is not quite the end of the story, as source C shows.

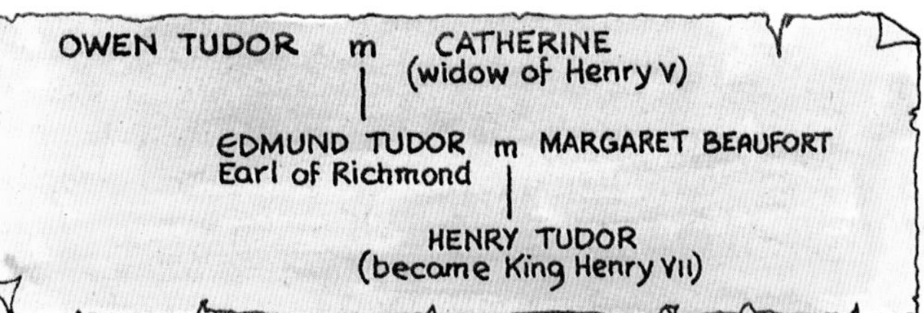

C This is the family tree of the Tudors.

Owen Tudor was a distant relative of Owain Glyndŵr. He married Henry V's widow, Catherine. Their grandson, Henry Tudor, was born at Pembroke Castle in 1457. He grew up in France.

In 1485, he came back to England at the head of an army. Many of his supporters were Welsh. That same year, he defeated King Richard II at the Battle of Bosworth Field. A man with a Welsh grandfather was now King of England.

Many Welsh people saw Henry's success as a Welsh victory. They hoped he would give Wales back its independence. It did not happen. Henry's son, Henry VIII, actually united England and Wales.

1 a) What part did these play in Welsh history: (a) Llywelyn, (b) Edward I and (c) Owain Glyndŵr?
b) Did each help the Welsh? Give reasons.

2 a) Read source D. Which monk wrote which poem? Give reasons.
b) Draw two columns on your page. Put the titles **Welsh view** and **English view** on your columns. Now, write down the words which each monk used to describe Llywelyn.
b) Find at least one pair of words where they disagree completely.
c) Does this mean that one of the writers must have been wrong? Give reasons.

3 a) You are a Welsh person in the Middle Ages. How do you *feel* when you look at source E?
b) You are an English person in the Middle Ages. How do *you* feel when you look at source E?
c) Now, look at source D again. How do your answers compare with what the monks wrote?
d) Do you think people are bound to be biased when talking about war? Give reasons.

D These contemporary poems were recorded by William Rishanger in *Chronicles and Annals*. One poem was written by an English monk; the other was written by a Welsh monk.

Here lies the **scourge** of England,
Snowdonia's guardian sure,
Llywelyn, prince of Wales,
In character most pure.
Of modern kings the jewel,
Of kings long past the flower,
For kings to come a pattern,
Radiant in lawful power.

Here lies the prince of errors,
A traitor and a thief,
A flaring, flaming firebrand,
The **malefactors'** chief.
The wild Welsh evil genius,
Who sought the good to kill,
Dregs of the faithless Trojans,
And source of every ill.

Sources are often biased. People writing about a war often support one side or the other. Historians have to compare these sources to get a balanced view.

E This monument at Cilmery is supposed to mark the spot where Llywelyn died in 1282.

16 CHANGE AND CONTINUITY

The Normans were the last people to invade Britain and win. By the time Henry Tudor became king, much had changed. Throughout that time, people tried to improve their lives.

So the Middle Ages brought much in the way of progress. Some new ideas were simple, such as forks and handkerchiefs. But there was also complicated new machinery, such as the windmill. People re-discovered things which had been forgotten. Some buildings were made of bricks – the first since Roman times.

Changes do not always bring progress. Norman laws took away some of the freedom which Saxon women were used to. Before 1066, a free Saxon woman could own her own property. Under the Normans, her husband was her lord. If she wished to make a gift, she had to ask him.

Many peasants, too, were worse off. Before 1066, most people had been free. It was William I who introduced the feudal system which took away the peasants' freedom. From then on, their lives were controlled by their lord. Some still were in 1485.

These peasants now had to take their corn to be ground in the lord's mill – and pay for the privilege. In Saxon times, they had ground corn at home, using a quern .

The Abbot of St Albans had seized the peasants' grindstones to make sure people used the mill. He used the stones to make a floor for his house. When the peasants revolted in 1381, the St Albans peasants made sure they tore them all up.

What were they like, these peasants of all those years ago? Were they like us? Or have human beings changed, too, as years have passed?

We know they looked rather like us. Archaeologists dug up a graveyard in North Yorkshire. The men, they found, were 1.68 metres tall on average. But medieval people had fuller mouths than we do. Their jaw bones were stronger. They were more used to chewing coarse food than we are.

We also know that they lived shorter lives. The adult men in the Yorkshire graves were, on average, just over 35 years old when they died. The women were just over 31. The average person today can expect to live at least twice that long.

They thought differently to us, too. For instance, in the Middle Ages, it was quite normal to weep openly in public. But people thought that really loud laughter was a sin.

Clothes, too, changed. The captions explain how and why.

A Covering the seeds with soil. This picture from the Luttrell Psalter (1340) also shows a person scaring birds.

One person whose life changed in 1066 was Gytha. Her husband had been Earl of Hereford. People called him Ralph the Timid because he was frightened of the Welsh.

In 1066, she owned land at Blisworth, now in Northamptonshire. William the Conqueror took away her land and gave it to William Peverel, one of his chief supporters.

But for the ordinary folk in Blisworth, their daily life went on as before. Peasants got up with the sun in 1066. They were still getting up at dawn in 1485. They were out in the fields, planting, weeding or harvesting from dawn to dusk. Their children frightened off the birds.

Of course, the peasants did not write about this. So, how can we be sure that daily life did not change? The answer is that we have primary sources from later periods.

These sources show that people were still living much like this 400 years later. By then, villagers had oil lamps instead of candles to light their homes. But farming work still went on from dawn to dusk. People still got up at daybreak.

Much of the farmwork was still done by hand. Children gathered food for the pigs. Wives still helped out, especially at harvest time. All of them touched their cap when the squire went past. Even the word 'squire' went back to Norman times. Originally, he was someone who carried a knight's shield.

But what about those children scaring away the birds in 1066? By 1899, there had been one big change. They had to go to school until they were eleven. And after that?

Well, my grandfather left school in the late 19th century. He lived in a small Norfolk village. So, of course, his first job was on the land. He got paid 25p for his first week's work. You can probably guess what it was: he was out scaring birds.

B Change does not happen everywhere at the same time. These Russian peasants did not get their freedom until 1861.

1 In pairs, divide a page into two columns. On the left, write **Different**. On the right, put **Similar**. On the left, list those things which had changed between 1066 and 1485. On the right, list those things which had not changed. You can add to your list from earlier chapters.

2 The pair with the longest list could read it out so you can all compare your answers.

GLOSSARY

ancestor – a person from whom you are descended (eg your grandmother)
archaeologist – a person who studies the remains of the past
barbican – a building which defends a drawbridge
baron – an important nobleman
battlement – a wall at the top of a tower
blasphemy – words spoken against God
boon-work – work done at busy times, such as harvest. The lord provided board (meals)
brethren – brothers (other monks)
burgess – a person who lived in a town which had a charter
burgh – a Scottish town with its own charter
census – an official count of a country's population
charter – a list of rights
chronicle – a history of events
chronological – in the order in which the events happened
conquest – an event in which a country is taken by force
contagion – a disease spread by touching
contemporaries – people who lived at the same time
creditor – someone to whom money or goods are owed
customs duty – a tax paid on goods brought into or taken out of the country
decade – ten years
epilepsy – a disease which causes fits
excommunicated – not allowed to be a member of the Church any longer
export – something sent out of the country
feudal system – system by which people gave services to their lord in return for land and protection
freeman – a person who was free of all (or most) duties to a lord
Gaelic – ancient language of Scotland and Ireland
gibbet – a post from which people were hanged
guild – a society for craftspeople and merchants
high treason – a crime against your monarch or your country
import – an article brought into the country
Interdict – a ban on church services by the Pope
invasion – an act of entering a country as an enemy
law – a rule made by a monarch or a government
leprosy – a disease which eats away the body
loyalty – faithfulness
malefactor – a criminal
manuscript – a book or paper written by hand
mark – 66.5p
martyr – a person who dies because of what he or she believes in
medieval – anything to do with the Middle Ages
miracle – an event which is against the laws of nature
monarch – a king or queen. A country ruled by a king or queen is called a monarchy
monastery – a building where monks or nuns lived
mosaic – a picture made of small stones
noble – a lord or lady
ordeal – a test of innocence
overlord – a lord with power over another lord
peasant – a poor farmer
pilgrimage – a journey to a holy place
pillory – a wooden frame with holes for the hands and head
Pope – the head of the Catholic Church
population – the number of people (living somewhere)
quern – a stone mill, worked by hand
refectory – a room for meals
relic – something belonging to a holy person
scourge – a person who causes great trouble
sheriff – a county official
shrine – a holy place
tenant – a person living on someone else's land
traitor – a person who betrays their monarch or country
vow – a solemn promise
woe – great misery